MORPH PIVOT LAUNCH™

NAVIGATE YOUR JOB SEARCH IN TURBULENT TIMES

WORKBOOK AND GUIDED JOURNAL

MORPH PIVOT LAUNCH™

NAVIGATE YOUR JOB SEARCH IN TURBULENT TIMES

WORKBOOK AND GUIDED JOURNAL

DEB GAUT

ILLUSTRATED BY

BONNIE SALES

boomatally press

Deb dedicates this book to

My amazing husband David, the love and light of my life

Bonnie dedicates this book to

Pat Holm, who taught me not to just let life happen
Deb Gaut, for believing in me
My True Self, who has grown into the woman and artist
I've always dreamt I could be

Contents

The Tumblewing as Our Muse

When was the last time you marveled at a colorful kite dancing effortlessly in the wind? Or gazed in wonder at a single leaf gently drifting and twirling in the breeze?

At these moments, both the kite and the leaf became little-known aeronautical phenomena known as *tumblewings*.

According to the language god Wikipedia, tumblewings "generate lift by alternately flying and stalling as the angle of incidence changes with the spinning motion."

They are nature's version of modern gliders, leveraging the power of the wind.

While writing this book, we learned about tumblewings and were instantly captivated. In fact, these marvelous wonders became our muse.

Rather than fighting the wind, tumblewings harness the wind to launch, glide, tumble, and roll.

They offer us valuable life lessons about using the power of the wind to propel us forward rather than hold us back.

For that reason, you will see illustrations of tumblewings throughout the book.

We hope their presence will offer you a sense of peace, hope, and inspiration in these difficult times.

A Short Introduction

Changing jobs or careers can be stressful, even in the best of times. Add a traumatic life event—separation or divorce, death of a spouse or partner, unexpected job loss—or a large-scale, far-reaching calamity—economic downturn, catastrophic weather event, or worldwide health crisis—and what was already a stressful process can become a terrifying proposition that feels impossible to navigate.

And Heaven forbid if more than one of these stressors hit at the same time.

Now, imagine having a professional career coach with you every step of the way—someone to help you manage the process, find your footing, and remain firm on your path to success.

That's what you have in this workbook and guided journal.

Using the coaching tools and techniques that I've learned, developed, and successfully applied as a Certified Professional Coach (CPC), *Morph, Pivot, Launch™* takes you through specific steps to help you

- Master your mindset
- Energize your job search
- Hold fast to your dreams

Through the exercises here, we'll work together, focusing on ways to marshal and sustain your energy and maintain your engagement while you develop and implement an effective job search strategy. We'll also work on articulating your dreams, wishes, and vision for yourself, and help you keep them centered in your sights as you plan for the future. To lessen your anxiety and stress and improve your overall state of mind, our gifted artist and illustrator Bonnie Sales has designed *Morph, Pivot, Launch™* with plenty of clever and engaging art throughout. Feel free to use this space to doodle, color, draw, and get your brain firing creatively.

There are many excellent books on the market about landing a job or changing careers. What this book uniquely offers is a bundled workbook, guidebook, organizer, journal, and reference manual—all in one—designed to coordinate together to help you set your course and reach your goal.

Whether you're 20-something, 70-something, or anywhere in between, this book is for you if difficulties beyond your control are driving your job or career change, or if the process itself is creating excessive turbulence in your life. Feel free to work through the book from cover to cover, or complete the exercises as needed. In the process, you'll be documenting your journey and writing your own personal story.

Changing jobs or careers *is* extraordinarily stressful. Our goal in creating *Morph, Pivot Launch™* is to help you go farther and faster with less stress and more joy. You can do this.

We believe in you!

Deb Gaut & Bonnie Sales

Master Your Mindset

Section I

Who Is the Person You Need to Become to Navigate a Crisis and Move Boldly Toward Your Dreams?

In times of extraordinary stress and uncertainty, our dreams for the future can feel impossible to achieve. Yet, these dreams have the potential to propel us forward in incredibly powerful ways—especially in times of personal, professional, or financial turmoil. So, the question becomes: *Who is the person you need to become to navigate your own crisis and move boldly toward your dreams?*

Think about this important question for a moment.

If you dream of running a marathon and have never run more than a couple of miles as your longest distance, you will need to become *someone who thinks, plans, trains, and acts like a marathoner.* You will need to become someone who is

1. 100% dedicated to achieving your goal

2. Aware of the mindset required for successful, long-distance runs

3. Smart about planning a long-distance training program

4. Committed to eating a nutritious diet, hydrating appropriately, and getting a good night's sleep regularly

5. Extraordinarily disciplined in executing your training plan

6. Dedicated to cross-training to build strength and endurance

7. Knowledgeable about the right gear to purchase (and use) to avoid injury and overcome the elements (e.g., weather, terrain, etc.)

8. Savvy about race preparation

9. Willing to prioritize marathon training at the top of your list

10. Exceptionally patient, as you'll need at least a year of experience running 3–4 times per week to establish a proper foundation before even starting a marathon-training program

Thought-provoking, right?

Think about your dreams for the future and brainstorm the traits, characteristics, and behaviors of the *person you will need to become* to navigate the crisis you're experiencing and make your dreams a reality. Be thorough and specific with the details. Use the space below to capture your brainstorming session.

To weather the storm and accomplish my dreams, I will need to become someone who....

1.

2.

3.

4.

5.

6.

7.

8.

9.

10.

How does completing this exercise affect the way that you think about your goals and dreams for the future? How determined are you to take on the challenge?

What changes in your mindset will you need to practice in order to get your journey off to a good start and sustain forward movement over the long term?

What new habits will you need to establish and practice regularly to accomplish your goals and dreams?

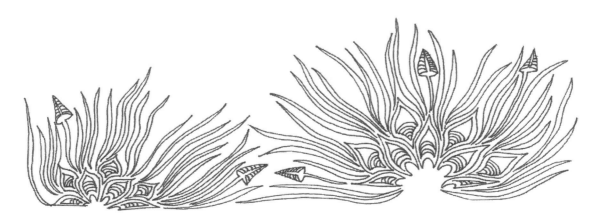

It's All About the Talk

A job search can be exciting, exasperating, exhausting, and so many other colorful words in the English language—especially in difficult times. What five words would you use to describe your own experiences with the job search process at this moment?

_____   _____   _____

_____   _____

Of the five descriptors that you identified above, how many are positive terms? _____
How many are negative terms? _____

The words we use in everyday life have a funny way of shaping the world as we perceive it, including our job search. In fact, our language can influence the extent to which we *thrive* rather than merely survive the process.

So, here are two important questions. Be specific with your answers.

1. What makes you think you CAN'T *thrive* while navigating your job search?

_____

_____

_____

_____

2. Now, what makes you think you CAN?   _____

_____

_____

_____

_____

Keep a close watch on the language you use throughout the day. Give yourself kudos when you catch yourself using positive self-talk and find a way to reframe negative self-talk to create a positive mindset.

Maximize Your Energy and Engagement*

"Your beliefs become your thoughts, your thoughts become your words, your words become your actions, your actions become your habits, your habits become your values, your values become your destiny."

— Mahatma Gandhi

According to the Institute for Professional Excellence in Coaching (iPEC), humans are driven by two types of energy: catabolic (destructive) energy, which holds us back, and anabolic (constructive) energy, which propels us forward. These two kinds of energy can be further divided into seven levels, each of which is defined by specific core thoughts, feelings, and actions.[1] How many of the seven energy levels presented in the table below do you recognize in yourself as relates to your job search?

Catabolic (Destructive) Energy

Energy Level	Core Thought	Core Feeling	Core Action
Level 1	*Victim* "Nothing ever goes right for me."	*Apathy* "How can I possibly work on my job search today?"	*Lethargy* Little or no forward movement; feeling defeated, stuck, overwhelmed
Level 2	*Conflict* "Please stop. I don't need or want your help or advice."	*Anger* "I feel agitated and angry when you try to tell me what to do."	*Defiance* Short bursts of energy; being judgmental, demanding, overbearing

---

* *The content in this discussion contains my interpretation of the copyrighted work of Bruce D. Schneider and the Institute for Professional Excellence in Coaching. Source: iPEC. (2016, 2017a). COR.E Transitions Dynamics: Foundations Client Workbook, pp. 46-56.*

Anabolic (Constructive) Energy

Energy Level	Core Thought	Core Feeling	Core Action
Level 3	*Responsibility* "I need to step up my game this week."	*Forgiveness* "I forgive myself for taking a break yesterday. Today's a new day."	*Cooperation* Reaching out for help, seeing solutions, compromising
Level 4	*Concern* "Enough about me. How are you today?"	*Compassion* "It's perfectly understandable that we're both feeling stressed."	*Service* Being kind, caring, empathetic; serving others
Level 5	*Reconciliation* "Life is what we make of it. What good things can come from this situation?"	*Peace* "I feel peaceful, passionate, curious, excited, and motivated."	*Acceptance* Accepting my situation, seeing opportunities all around me
Level 6	*Synthesis* "We're all in this together. What can we create from this situation that will serve us all?"	*Joy* "I feel happy, joyous, and in the zone."	*Wisdom* Experiencing a connection with everyone and everything
Level 7	*Non-judgment* "Life itself is neither good nor bad. Living life to the fullest is why we're here."	*Absolute Passion* "I feel completely alive, and I'm living in the moment."	*Creation* Genius thinking, brilliant ideas, unconditional love

What's fascinating about this approach to understanding our energy is the argument that *our thoughts drive our feelings, and our feelings drive our actions.* For example, if we think of ourselves as victims of our situation, then we will feel and act like victims (Level 1). However, if we generate thoughts that reflect a higher level of energy, such as concern for others (Level 4), then our feelings (compassion) and actions (service) will follow.

So, what does this information have to do with job seeking? The answer is, "Everything," when it comes to your *engagement* with the process. The higher your energy level, the greater your engagement level. The greater your engagement level, the more power and choice you have over your life.[2]

To illustrate, consider the following range of engagement that you may experience with job-seeking tasks (e.g., searching for positions online, updating your resume, asking for referrals, networking via Zoom, etc.). The left side of the scale reflects low engagement, and the right side with high engagement.[3]

"Won't do it." →	"Have to do it." →	"Need to do it." →	"Choose to do it."
No power	Force	Low power	High power
No choice	Limited to no choice	Mostly by choice	Total choice

[Source: iPEC (2016, 2017b). COR.E Transitions Dynamics: Influencer's Client Workbook, p. 9.]

When you're engaged with a task, you're attracted to it, emotionally involved with it, and excited to make it happen. The higher you are on the range of engagement, the more willing, enthusiastic, and motivated you are to do the work.

Again, the higher your energy level, the higher your engagement level. The two are inextricably linked.

So, how can you improve your energy AND engagement levels, especially if you're experiencing exceptionally elevated anxiety and stress?

Keep working your way through this workbook, and we'll show you how!

Aha Moments

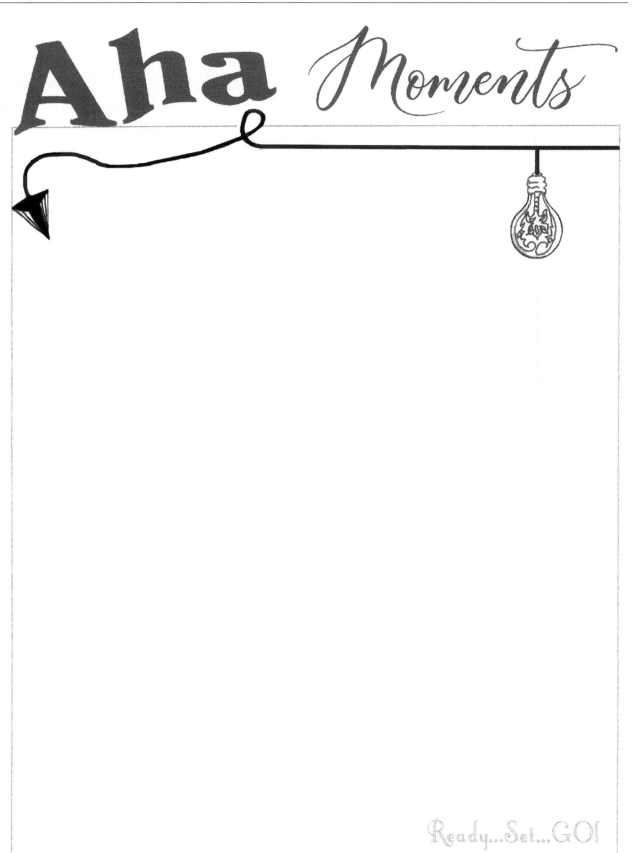

Ready...Set...GO!

The Ten Most Common Challenges We Face When Navigating Major Life Changes

According to iPEC, one of the top training programs for coaches in the world, the ten most common challenges we face when navigating major life changes are:

_____ 1. Loss of self-confidence

_____ 2. Consistently stressful feelings

_____ 3. Decreased enjoyment of life

_____ 4. Inability to focus and adapt to change

_____ 5. Trouble performing well under pressure

_____ 6. Issues managing time and balancing work and life

_____ 7. Problems defining and achieving goals

_____ 8. Difficulties implementing strategies

_____ 9. Undermining yourself when making decisions or taking action

_____ 10. No effective plan to create positive change[4]

To establish a baseline of where you are right now as relates to your job or career change, please rate the extent to which you're experiencing each of these challenges using the following five-point scale:

1 = Very Little

2 = Little

3 = Some

4 = Great

5 = Very Great

Use the space to the left of each challenge above to record your rating. Once you've assigned your ratings, go back and identify the top three challenges in the list that are causing you anxiety and stress, and copy them in the space below:

1. _____

2. _____

3. _____

In the following exercise, we'll conduct a "deep dive" into each of these challenges and explore several options for addressing them.

You Always Have Five Choices

Whether or not you are aware of the alternatives when dealing with problems or challenges, you ALWAYS, ALWAYS, ALWAYS have five choices. You can

1. Suffer and remain a victim to the situation
2. Avoid the situation
3. Change the situation or bring it closer to a resolution
4. Alter your experience of the situation by looking at it from a different perspective
5. Accept the situation, knowing that things will be different in a week, month, or year[5,6]

Think about the incredible power of this information for virtually every situation—even when stress and anxiety are running high. How does it make you feel to know you always have five choices?

To test this knowledge for yourself, let's take a "deep dive" into the top three challenges that you identified in the prior exercise.

Start by copying your greatest challenge into the space below. Then, place a check mark in the box that best represents the primary way that you're currently choosing to approach that challenge. (Note: You'll complete the same process for all three challenges.)

1. Challenge #1: _____

   ☐ Suffering—embracing my inner victim
   ☐ Avoiding the situation
   ☐ Changing the situation to bring it closer to resolution
   ☐ Altering my experience of the situation by looking at it from a different perspective
   ☐ Accepting the situation unconditionally, knowing things will be different in the future

   On a scale of 1–5, how well is this choice working for you?

   _____ 1 = Not working at all

   _____ 2 = A little

   _____ 3 = Some

   _____ 4 = Well

   _____ 5 = Very well

   If your score is less than 5, which of the four remaining choices would you be willing to try for the next 7–10 days to address this challenge?

   Your new choice: _____

What plan could you put into place to increase your chances for success?

_____

_____

_____

2. Challenge #2: _____

☐ Suffering—embracing my inner victim
☐ Avoiding the situation
☐ Changing the situation to bring it closer to resolution
☐ Altering my experience of the situation by looking at it from a different perspective
☐ Accepting the situation unconditionally, knowing things will be different in the future

Once again, on a scale of 1–5, how well is this choice working to your advantage?

_____ 1 = Not working at all
_____ 2 = A little
_____ 3 = Some
_____ 4 = Well
_____ 5 = Very well

If your choice is less than 5, which of the four remaining choices would you like to try for the next 7–10 days to address this challenge?

Your new choice: _____

What plan could you put into place to increase your chances for success?

_____

_____

_____

3. Challenge #3: _____

☐ Suffering—embracing my inner victim
☐ Avoiding the situation
☐ Changing the situation to bring it closer to resolution
☐ Altering my experience of the situation by looking at it from a different perspective
☐ Accepting the situation unconditionally, knowing things will be different in the future

You know the drill.

On a scale of 1–5, how well is this choice working for you?

_____ 1 = Not working at all

_____ 2 = A little

_____ 3 = Some

_____ 4 = Well

_____ 5 = Very well

If your score is less than 5, which of the four remaining choices would you like to try for the next 7–10 days to address this challenge?

Your new choice: _____

What plan could you put into place to increase your chances for success?

_____

_____

_____

_____

So, what do you think? Are you ready to put one or more of your new game plans into action?

_____

How are you feeling now that you know you always have five choices?

_____

_____

_____

If you're feeling courageous (it's OK if you're not), share your top three challenges and game plans for addressing them with a trusted friend or colleague—someone who is willing to serve as your *accountability partner.*

Being accountable for your actions with someone whom you trust and admire is a powerful way to ensure that you stay strong and implement any game plan you choose to pursue.

Who could serve as your accountability partner as you move forward with your job search?

Write this person's name here: _____

Now, jot down the exact date and time when you will reach out and ask for his or her help. (You could offer to serve in the same role for him or her.)

Date: _____   Time: _____

Now, take a big gulp and make the call.

Problems and Challenges, or Opportunities?

"A company once sent two shoe salespeople to an area in Africa where they had never sold any shoes. One was their senior, most experienced salesman, Tom, and they expected big things of him.

The other was an optimistic rookie named Cynthia. She didn't have much experience, but she had a lot of enthusiasm. They figured she might be able to sell a few pair of shoes.

Shortly after their arrival in Africa, Tom, the experienced salesperson, wrote the home office saying, 'You might as well bring me back. Nobody here wears shoes.'

The rookie, Cynthia, wired the home office an urgent message: 'Send me all the shoes you've got. Nobody here is wearing shoes!' " 7

This powerful story underscores the extraordinary difference in perspectives that can drive how we see and approach our daily lives and careers. Where one person sees only problems and challenges that are too great to overcome, another sees opportunities and possibilities to be embraced and pursued with gusto. The key to success is the ability to switch perspectives and to see the world through the prism of opportunity as often as possible. Not yet a believer? Try the following exercise in relation to your job search, and we'll talk about what you observed and experienced at the end of the activity.

Take the next few minutes and jot down a specific problem that you are facing in your job search. (Examples: *How am I supposed to a find job when I've spent the past 20 years building my own restaurant business?* Or *I have submitted more than 100 job applications online, and nobody has responded.)* Make a few notes about your problem here:

What emotions are you experiencing as you think about this challenge?

Now, imagine yourself working for several hours on tasks associated with your job search with this specific challenge swirling in your head.

- How would these negative thoughts affect your feelings and actions?

- How would these negative thoughts affect your energy and engagement with the tasks you're attempting to accomplish?

Now, close your eyes for a few minutes and clear your mind completely.

Relax your body, and take five (5) slow, deep breaths.

Once you've completely relaxed and banished these negative thoughts, turn your attention to three *opportunities* that a job or career change offers you (e.g., "an exciting, new career

Morph, Pivot, Launch™

adventure" or "the chance to truly shine in a new job or career"). Really dig into the possibilities and unleash your imagination. You can write the opportunities here:

1. _____
   _____
2. _____
   _____
3. _____
   _____

To what extent were you able to experience a very real "cognitive switch" as you began to brainstorm potential opportunities? Please explain.

What emotions did you experience as a function of your positive thoughts about these opportunities?

Now, imagine working for several hours on your job search with these opportunities at the forefront of your mind.

- How would these positive thoughts affect your feelings and actions?

Copyright ©2021 Boomalally LLC. All rights reserved.

- How would these positive thoughts affect your energy and engagement with the tasks you want to complete?

As we mentioned earlier, remember that *our thoughts drive our feelings, and our feelings drive our actions—and results*. Keeping this three-step process in mind will go a long way toward helping you shift perspectives and leverage the many opportunities that you can create.

Random Thoughts
Ready...Set...GO!

Lessons learned

ideas

Brainstorm

WISHES

desires

GOALS

What Influences Our Energy and Engagement?

"Our greatest glory is not in never falling, but in rising every time we fall"

— Confucius

Six factors play significant roles in our energy and engagement levels at any given moment:

1) Spiritual factors – the extent to which we're honoring our sense of purpose, beliefs, aims, values, and talents with a particular activity

2) Mental factors – anything that affects our sense of clarity and focus, level of interest, and perceived challenge associated with an activity

3) Physical factors – mindfulness regarding our bodies and how well we're taking care of ourselves, including getting enough sleep and nourishment; exercising consistently and managing our weight; and preventing or treating medical conditions

4) Emotional factors – degree to which an activity fits with our needs and desires; strikes the right amount of balance vs. tension in our lives; satisfies our thirst for novelty and excitement; and allows us to feel a sense of control or choice

5) Social factors – the quality and quantity of our interactions; amount of support that we receive from others; preferences for the types of people who surround us (e.g., individual vs. team players); and status/health of current relationships

6) Environmental factors – elements of the environment that enhance or detract from what we're doing, e.g., temperature (too hot, too cold); amount and quality of light; beauty and functionality of the space in which we're living or working; and level of noise (too much or too little)[8]

In the following pages, take a few minutes and make notes about specific elements of these six "influencers" that are affecting your job search this week.

Then, list three to five specific changes that you could make which would maximize, minimize, or leverage these factors to increase your energy and engagement with your daily work.

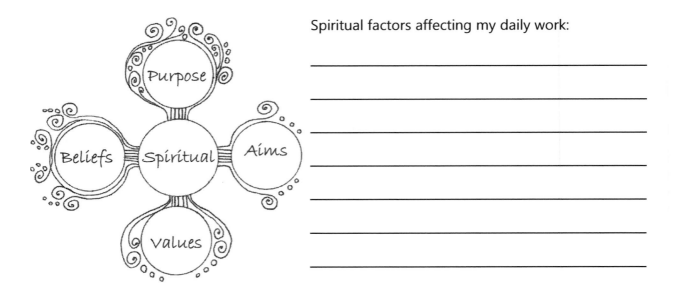

Spiritual factors affecting my daily work:

_____

_____

_____

_____

_____

_____

_____

Things I can do to better align my job search with my purpose, beliefs, aims, values, and talents (e.g., focus my search on companies whose values align with my own; research ways prospective companies give back to their communities):

1.

2.

3.

4.

5.

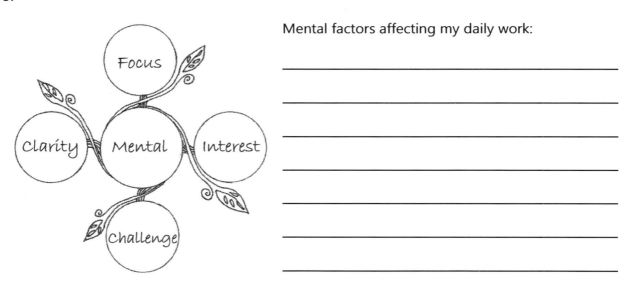

Mental factors affecting my daily work:

_____

_____

_____

_____

_____

_____

_____

Things I can do to increase my clarity, focus, and interest level, and optimize my desired level of challenge during the job-search process (e.g., ask three friends to help me expand my network rather than going it alone):

1.

2.

3.

4.

5.

Physical factors affecting my daily work:

_____

_____

_____

_____

_____

_____

_____

Fuel

Sleep Physical Illness & Injury

Exercise

Things I can do to be more mindful of my body and take better care of myself, including getting enough sleep and nourishment; consistently exercising and managing my weight; and preventing or treating medical conditions (e.g., practice yoga daily to improve my energy and vitality):

1.

2.

3.

4.

5.

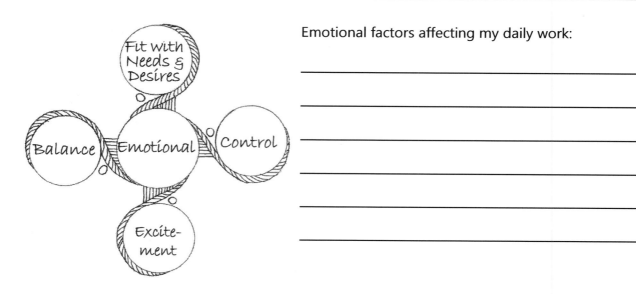

Emotional factors affecting my daily work:

_____

_____

_____

_____

_____

_____

Things I can do to achieve greater alignment with my needs and desires, preferred level of balance vs. tension in life, thirst for novelty and excitement, and sense of control and choice (e.g., spend quality time with my family every day; plan my work and work my plan):

1.

2.

3.

4.

5.

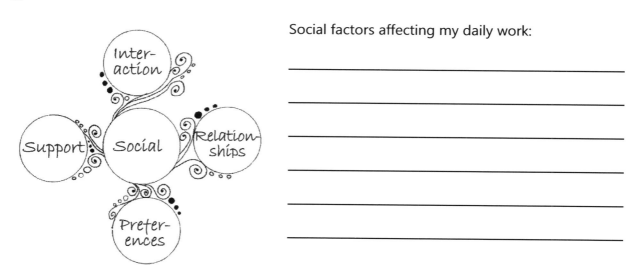

Social factors affecting my daily work:

_____

_____

_____

_____

_____

_____

Things I can do to improve the quality and quantity of my interactions, maximize the level of support I receive from others, make the most of people who surround me, and optimize the health of my current relationships (e.g., avoid isolating; seek networking opportunities with likeminded people):

1.

2.

3.

4.

5.

Environmental factors affecting my daily work:

_____

_____

_____

_____

_____

_____

Things I can do to improve my environment, including controlling temperature; amount and quality of light; beauty and functionality of the space in which I live and work; and level of noise (e.g., purchase a new desk lamp and ergonomic desk chair; tidy up my desk; negotiate an agreeable schedule with my kids that keeps the noise level in check while I'm working):

1.

2.

3.

4.

5.

Think of your energy and engagement levels as a glass of cool, refreshing water. Throughout your day, the amount of water in your glass rises and falls, depending on your spiritual, mental, physical, emotional, social, and environmental well-being.

When you become aware that one of the six factors is out of alignment, stop and consider what you can do to leverage that factor to your advantage.

In the process, you will increase not only your energy and engagement, but also your efficiency, effectiveness, and overall satisfaction with your job search.

Taming Your GAILs

GAILs are powerful energy blocks that take four different forms: Gremlins, Assumptions, Interpretations, and Limiting Beliefs.[9] They can be our worst enemies when it comes to managing our energy and engagement during a job or career change. These exercises are designed to introduce you to your GAILS and help you develop ways to tame them.*

I. Gremlins

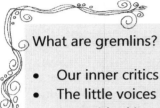

What are gremlins?

- Our inner critics
- The little voices in our heads that tell us to avoid taking risks and trying things (both old and new)
- Results: Compromises in life and playing "small"[10]

Examples:

- "I'm not smart enough to get this job."
- "I'm not savvy enough to publish Facebook or LinkedIn live videos."
- "I'm too old to follow my passion and become an artist."
- "I'm too inexperienced to be a successful entrepreneur."

Your turn: What gremlins are playing fast and loose in your head? Fill in the blanks:

"I'm not _____ enough to
_____"

"I'm not _____ enough to
_____"

"I'm too _____
to _____"

"I'm too _____
to _____"

In what ways are each of your gremlins affecting your energy, engagement, and productivity (e.g., lack of energy and motivation, disinterest in life and relationships, feelings of helplessness and hopelessness)? Use the space on the following page to make a few notes.

---

* *This four-part exercise is based on my interpretation of the copyrighted work of Bruce D. Schneider and the Institute for Professional Excellence in Coaching (iPEC).*

Gremlin #1 Effects:

Gremlin #2 Effects:

Gremlin #3 Effects:

Gremlin #4 Effects:

Gremlins are often the most difficult energy blocks to overcome because they're based on negative past experiences and serve as early warning signals to keep us safe. The best way to reduce the power of a gremlin is to identify its existence, then see it as only one part of who you are, not your entire identity.[11]

Instead of beating yourself up, acknowledge your gremlin for its service in keeping you safe. Then tell that little voice, "It's understandable that you feel this way, gremlin. However, I have assessed the risks. The benefits outweigh the costs. We've got this – no sweat."[12]

What powerful messages could you craft for each of your gremlins to reduce their power over your ability to make conscious choices and live the life you want to lead? Be creative with this part of the activity. Go ahead! Speak directly to your gremlins.

Message to Gremlin #1:

Message to Gremlin #2:

Message to Gremlin #3:

Message to Gremlin #4:

II. Assumptions

What are assumptions?

- Beliefs in the form of predictions that something will happen in the future because it has happened in the past
- Results: Allowing our past to control our future[13]

Examples:

- "The last time I tried to get a job with Company A, I didn't get the job. If I try again, I know I'll fail."
- "My last interview was really stressful. The next one will be no better."
- "I tried unsuccessfully to take out a small-business loan a year ago. If I try again, the same thing will happen."

Your turn: What assumptions are you making about yourself and your career change based on past experiences, which may be holding you back from moving forward with confidence and power?

1. _____
   _____
   _____

2. _____
   _____
   _____

3. _____
   _____
   _____

In what specific ways are each of your assumptions adversely affecting your energy, engagement, and productivity with daily, career-related tasks (e.g., constantly swirling in Level 1 energy, little tolerance for risk, chronic fatigue, feelings of helplessness, etc.)?

- Assumption #1 Effects:

  _____
  _____
  _____

- Assumption #2 Effects:

  _____
  _____
  _____

- Assumption #3 Effects:

_____

_____

_____

According to iPEC, assumptions can be tricky to manage because they're grounded in personal experience and, therefore, involve more emotion and energy. They also can be deeply flawed. The main question to ask when challenging assumptions is, "Just because that happened in the past, why must it happen again in the future?"[14]

The next time you think something won't work based on your past experience, recognize your assumption for what it is, question it, and consciously choose to let it go and to take positive action.[15]

III. Interpretations

What are interpretations?

- Stories we tell ourselves about something that happens (or is said), and for which we look for confirming evidence to support our stories or explanations
- Results: Potentially flawed or biased interpretations[16]

Examples:

- "I know the interviewer didn't like me. She looked at me like I was nuts when I told her why I was perfect for the job."
- "I dressed way too formally for that Zoom event. I know they thought I didn't belong. I'm never going back."
- "When I called and asked about the job opening, the person who answered the phone was really rude. What a terrible place that must be to work."

Your turn: Look back over the past couple of days or weeks and identify two or three instances when you came to negative conclusions based on the stories you told yourself about someone or something that happened. Jot a few notes here:

1. _____
   _____
   _____

2. _____
   _____
   _____

3. _____
   _____
   _____

For each of the instances you identified above, what story (or explanation) did you tell yourself about what happened? How did your interpretation of events affect your energy and engagement at the time?

- Instance #1:

- Instance #2:

- Instance #3:

Two excellent ways to avoid potentially flawed or biased interpretations are (1) to simply observe and process events without making positive or negative judgments, and (2) to actively consider other perspectives or viewpoints that could equally explain your observations.[17] Consider the following alternative interpretations of the three examples provided in the table on the previous page:

- "The interviewer smiled when I told her why I was perfect for the job. I wonder what she was thinking when she smiled."
- "I dressed way too formally for that Zoom event, allowed myself to feel out of place, and avoided making contributions. Next time I'll dress appropriately, and my confidence will improve."
- "When I called and asked about the job opening, the person who answered the phone spoke with a voice that seemed stressed. I wonder what was going on for him at that moment."

How could you reframe your interpretations of the two or three incidents that you shared in this exercise to reduce the chances of flawed or biased interpretations? To what extent can you feel your energy and engagement levels shift when you reframe these events?

- Reframe #1:

- Reframe #2:

- Reframe #3:

IV. Limiting Beliefs

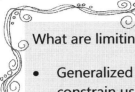

What are limiting beliefs?

- Generalized beliefs about the world that constrain us from moving forward with choice, power, and resolution; generally, they're learned from people whom we perceive to be credible (e.g., parents, teachers, religious leaders, the media)
- Results: Being unwilling to try new things or take risks, based solely on our limiting beliefs[18]

Examples:

- "Women will never be paid as much as men in the workplace. Why bother trying to negotiate the salary I know I deserve?"
- "People who are older than 50 cannot compete with younger job seekers. I'm 57. I'm not even going to try and submit an application and risk rejection."

Your turn: Take a few moments to identify any limiting beliefs that may be affecting your job search or career change. Feel free to make notes here:

1. _____
_____
_____

2. _____
_____
_____

3. _____
_____
_____

Here are five steps you can take to challenge or assess the truth (i.e., validity and reliability) of limiting beliefs:

(1) Identify any beliefs you hold that may be standing in your way of moving forward.
(2) Assess how those beliefs have affected or influenced your thoughts, feelings, and actions (or inaction)—and the outcomes of those actions.
(3) Explore the sources of your information regarding your limiting beliefs to assess the credibility of evidence that was offered to support those claims.
(4) Search for direct evidence or proof that the beliefs are true or false.
(5) Based on the outcomes of your exploration, modify your limiting beliefs or develop new beliefs that you can consciously and deliberately test for success in your own life.[19]

What do you think? Are you willing to give it a try?

- Choose one limiting belief that is standing in your way of moving forward. Write that belief in the following space:

- How has this limiting belief affected or influenced your thoughts, feelings, and actions? What has been the outcome of your actions (or inaction)?

- What sources of information directly or indirectly informed this belief? What evidence (if any) do you remember being offered to support the claim?

- Where could you go for direct evidence or proof that your belief is true or false?

- Based on your research, what did you learn about your belief?

- How could you modify your belief or create a new belief to directly test for success in your own life?

As you can see, GAILS are major energy blocks that we need to overcome to move forward with energy and engagement.

So, what did you learn about yourself or your situation as a function of working through some of your own gremlins, assumptions, interpretations, and limiting beliefs?

How committed are you to increasing awareness of your GAILs given their extraordinary power to keep you from moving forward with grit, determination, and confidence? (1 = Low, 10 = High)

       1   2   3   4   5   6   7   8   9   10

If you answered this question with a score of less than 10, what would it take to move you at least one level higher on the commitment scale?

If you can increase your awareness and commitment to observing your GAILS, you can catapult yourself from catabolic to anabolic energy much easier. In the process, you can improve your energy and engagement, and increase your efficiency and effectiveness with the job-seeking process.

The Stories We Tell Ourselves

One of the most intriguing lessons that coaches learn to share early on with our clients is the enormous impact of stories we tell ourselves about the world around us. What makes this phenomenon truly remarkable is that we (as humans) do not respond emotionally to facts, but to the stories we tell ourselves about those facts. Please allow me to repeat this statement given its far-reaching implications. *We do not respond emotionally to facts, but to the stories we tell ourselves about those facts.*[20]

To illustrate, here are at least five different stories that could emerge from a specific communication exchange during the same job interview. Look for the GAILs that may be coloring the picture. You will see them identified in parentheses.

FACT: The interviewer smiled when I told her I'm right for the job.

Story #1: The interviewer likes me. She smiled when I told her I'm right for the job.
(*Interpretation #1 of the interviewer's smile*)

Story #2: The interviewer thinks I'm a total goofball. She smiled when I told her I'm right for the job.
(*Interpretation #2* of that same smile)

Story #3: I showed way too much enthusiasm for the job during my job interview. The interviewer smiled when I told her I'm right for the job.
(*Assumption* about what is appropriate or inappropriate to say during an interview → *Interpretation #3* of the smile)

Story #4: Men are much tougher than women as interviewers. The female interviewer responded much more warmly when I told her I'm right for the job.
(*Limiting belief* about men versus women interviewers → *Interpretation #4* of smile)

Story #5: I totally blew the interview. I am unworthy of the job. The interviewer laughed under her breath when I told her I'm right for the job.
(*Gremlin* about worthiness → *Interpretation #5* of smile)

Crazy but true. So, here's the most important question. What stories are you telling yourself—particularly negative stories—that may be coloring your perceptions and decreasing your energy around the job- or career-change process?

In the space below, let's dig into at least one recent communication exchange or incident related to your job search that triggered a negative story on your part in the past week. In the space below, see if you can articulate (a) the facts of the situation without any interpretations or judgments; (b) the story you told yourself about the facts; (c) the valence of the story—positive or negative; (d) any GAILs that could have colored your perceptions of the facts; and (e) how the story you told yourself made you feel and act afterwards.

Event: _____

- Just the facts:

_____

_____

_____

_____

- Story I told myself about the facts:

_____

_____

_____

_____

- My story was: _____ Positive   _____ Negative (check one)

- GAILs that may have colored my perceptions of the facts:

_____

_____

_____

_____

- How my story made me feel and act:

_____

_____

_____

_____

Powerful stuff, right?

Knowing what you know now, what *strategies* could you put into place that would help you to avoid telling yourself negative stories about people, situations, and communication exchanges that serve to decrease your energy and engagement? (Hint! Increasing your self-awareness and considering alternative perspectives, viewpoints, or interpretations of events might be a great place to begin.)

_____

_____

_____

_____

_____

In what ways could greater self-awareness about your own storytelling feats help to improve your energy and engagement?

_____

_____

_____

_____

_____

To what extent are you willing to give your newfound, story-busting strategies a try? (1 = That's a big fat no for me; 7 = That's a big, honking, crazy yes!)

1   2   3   4   5   6   7

Once again why or why not?

_____

_____

_____

_____

_____

Being Present in the Moment

"Realize deeply that the present moment is all you ever have. Make the Now the primary focus of your life."

— Eckhart Tolle

One of the most powerful coaching concepts that each of us can practice daily is being present in the moment. Doing so can make all the difference when it comes to reducing our stress and anxiety levels, even during the job- or career-change process.

Think about this simple, amazing concept for a moment. When was the last time you experienced a moment of sheer joy, happiness, and abandon – one which was so exhilarating that you can remember willing time to stand still? That experience is perhaps the best example of what it means to be present in the moment. You weren't thinking about anything else. You were simply living life full-out in that moment.

When we allow our thoughts to leave the present moment and dwell on the past or future, we can easily feel a loss of control.

To illustrate, think about a traumatic past event or time period that you experienced during a previous job or career.

What happened?

_____

_____

_____

_____

_____

When you think or talk with other people about this event or time period in your life, what feelings or emotions do you experience?

_____

_____

_____

_____

_____

Now for the big question: What happens to your energy as a function of these negative thoughts and feelings—especially when you're working on tasks related to finding your future job or career? To what extent do your thoughts and feelings affect your actions?

_____

_____

_____

_____

_____

Likewise, when you think about the coming weeks and months, what worries you the most?

_____

_____

_____

_____

What feelings or emotions do you experience when you think or talk about your worries and concerns?

_____

_____

_____

_____

How do these thoughts and feelings affect your actions in the now?

_____

_____

_____

_____

_____

What benefits would you experience if you practiced being present in the moment as you go about the business of finding a new job or career?

_____

_____

_____

_____

_____

On a scale of 1–10, how committed are you to practicing being present in the moment for the next 48 hours? (1 = Low, 10 = High)

1   2   3   4   5   6   7   8   9   10

Feel free to make notes below regarding what you learn about yourself or situation while trying this experiment.

Notes

Go Slower to Go Farther

One of the most compelling lessons that distance runners learn about running hills is the value of maintaining your *tempo* (beat or strike of your footfalls) and breathing *rhythm* (frequency of inhalation) but shortening your *stride* (distance between steps) while climbing a hill. Once you've topped the incline, you can return to your regular stride without having ever changed your tempo or breathing rhythm. Yes, your running time will increase as you scale the incline, but you can run much farther in the long run having avoided unnecessary exhaustion.

Interestingly, this phenomenon applies equally well to a job or career change, particularly when you're going through difficult times. Given the challenges you may be facing, the job search process can become the equivalent of a marathon training program.

So, what would practicing a *Go Slower to Go Farther* approach to job seeking look like? Remember your goal is to maintain your tempo and rhythm, but to take shorter strides. One example would be to set a goal of submitting three excellent, well-conceived job applications per day, rather than hustling to send out five or six hastily prepared applications. You would be spending the same amount of time during the day working on your job search (i.e., maintaining your tempo), but you would be doing so without rushing the process (i.e., changing your rhythm). By increasing the quality and decreasing the quantity of applications that you attempt to submit, you avoid running the risk of "burning out" before you cross the finish line and land the job.

In addition to the number of job applications that you may want to submit daily or weekly, what other tasks associated with your job search would benefit from a *Go Slower to Go Farther* approach? See if you can think of at least three such tasks and capture your notes here:

Task #1:

Task #2:

Task #3:

How do you feel now about the possibility of applying this approach as part of your own job-seeking strategy?

On a scale of 1–10, how committed are you to experimenting with this approach in the next 7–10 days? (1=Low, 10=High)

1   2   3   4   5   6   7   8   9   10

Why or why not?

Go Slower to Go Farther: Deb's Personal Story

I personally learned this valuable lesson from a kind, compassionate race coordinator during a miserable, rainy, frigid 5k race in the dead of winter in Saint Louis, Missouri. As I was trudging up one of the hills in the last mile of the race with no others in sight (everyone else had long finished), the race coordinator pulled up beside me in his car and graciously shared this brilliant piece of advice. And it worked! I ran the last few hills without having to catch my breath and finished the race. I will never, ever forget his kindness, nor his life-changing advice. In fact, his wise words helped us to complete this book in time to share it with you now.

Final Thoughts

Ready...Set...Go!

Energize Your Job Search

Section II

Take Time to Build Your Master Resume File

No matter whether times are good or bad, you must find ways to stand out from the crowd and show potential employers that you're right for the job. Your ability to custom tailor your job application for each position is vital to your success, especially now that many companies use applicant tracking systems and software (ATS) to "weed out" job applications that fail to closely match their job descriptions.

The idea of customizing your resume and cover letter for each position can be daunting without a good system for documenting your work experience. One way to reduce the angst and pain of the process is to develop a Master Resume File. If you're starting from scratch, the process of building such a file may seem tedious and time consuming. However, investing your time and energy NOW will earn maximum dividends: the ability to quickly and easily custom-tailor job applications and to take your job search to a whole new level.

At a minimum, your Master Resume File can take the form of a manila file folder or accordion file stored easily within reach. First, gather all pertinent information and add it to the folder. (See bulleted list below for information or items to include.) Whenever you complete an important task or project, achieve a significant milestone, or earn an award (e.g., "Employee of the Month"), simply add a dated, handwritten note to the file and include printed copies of documentation. Then, when it's time to update your resume—especially if it has been a while—you can limit the amount of time that's necessary to remember and document your accomplishments.

Even more effective is to create and store an electronic version of your Master Resume File on your computer's desktop. From there, you can easily update the file with quick notations, including specific dates and relevant information. Consider making electronic copies of documentation and storing these documents in the same location as your Master Resume File. To easily create a customized resume or cover letter, format your master file to look like an actual resume. (For example, capture information in bulleted form and list your experience in reverse chronological order.)

Sections to include are

- Work experience, including company name, job location, job title, and start/end dates
- Education, including name of institution, degree or certification completed, school location, and years attended (Note: If you're a recent grad, then document relevant coursework, societies, organizations, and extracurricular activities.)

- Skills, including projects in which you used those skills; specific accomplishments and outcomes associated with each project; years of experience with each skill; and level of expertise
- Awards and honors (e.g., "Customer Experience Innovation Award" or "Leadership Award")
- Volunteer work and organizations, especially work which uses skills that may be applicable to the kinds of jobs for which you're applying[21]

Don't worry about the length of your Master Resume File. It may be two, three, four, or more pages long. Your goal is to be thorough and comprehensive. (Note: You can easily review the file periodically to keep the information updated and fresh.)

Then, when you want to create a customized resume and cover letter for a specific job or position, you can easily

- block copy pertinent bullets from your master file to your customized resume or cover letter file
- order your bulleted content to reflect the order of requirements listed in the target job description
- edit the language of your bullets to match key words and phrases used in the job description
- date, save, and file your customized resume and cover letter by version
- get your custom-tailored job application out the door

How have you kept track of your job experience in the past (e.g., ongoing education, including courses and certifications; projects and specific outcomes; skills learned; accomplishments, awards, and honors; volunteer work, etc.)?

How well has that approach worked for you in the past when you wanted to apply for a new job or submit your qualifications for a promotion or award?

What are the advantages and disadvantages of creating and maintaining an updated Master Resume File?

How willing are you to give it a try? (1=Low; 10=High)   Your Score: _____

A Quick Way to Customize Your Resume

Depending on the amount of time you have available, you may need a quick and easy way to customize your job applications. In an excellent article entitled "Customize Your Resume to Stand Out from the Crowd," Charles Etorama offers a simple, effective five-step process:

1. Review job description
   - Look closely at job title; duties and responsibilities; job requirements; and job location
   - Make a list of all key terms for possible use in your own resume
2. Match job title listed in resume with job title included in description
   - Example: Chief Financial Officer, Maintenance Crew Lead
   - Place exact job title directly below your name on resume
3. Align skills with key terms in job description
   - Use employer's key terms when presenting your own skills and experiences to show how well you fit
   - If employer lists requirements in a specific order, then use that order to present your qualifications (1..., 2..., 3...)
4. Call attention to most important skills (for employer!) at top of resume
   - Create a box at top of resume that is 3–5 lines of vertical space
   - Use this space to highlight experience and achievements that fit most pertinent requirements
   - Name this section "Summary of Qualifications" or similar title
5. List your location if you live near job site
   - If you want to underscore that you live close to a job site, then add your city and state under your name
   - Avoid including physical mailing address[22]

What do you think? Interested in giving the process a test drive?

First, find a job description for a position in which you're interested in applying. (LinkedIn, Indeed, and Glass Door are three great job boards where you can search for potential jobs.)

Write the job title here: _____

Second, make a list of key terms that show up in the job description, particularly those that are mentioned more than once.

_____   _____   _____

_____   _____   _____

_____   _____   _____

_____   _____   _____

Third, read through your most recent resume. As you move through the resume, circle the experience, education, skills, and expertise that match well with the requirements listed in the job description.

Fourth, for purposes of this exercise, rewrite at least three or four bullets in your resume that match well with the job description using the key words that you identified in Step #2. Feel free to use the following space or create your own electronic version:

- _____

- _____

- _____

- _____

How well did the process work for you? What did you like most and least? How could you adjust the process to fit your needs?

How committed are you to using this simple process to begin customizing your resumes for your current job search? (1 = Not feeling it; 10 = Oh, yeah. Sign me up!)

1   2   3   4   5   6   7   8   9   10

What would it take to increase your commitment level by one or two steps?

"Job Hunting Tips to Beat ATS"
Guest Contributor: Kristen Edens

My earliest resume experience was in the late 1970s helping my father climb the corporate ladder. Every few years, my mother would type up an all-purpose resume and cover letter, make dozens of copies of THE SAME RESUME, and send it to several job openings across the country. My contribution was to type the addresses onto the envelopes, stuff the envelopes, then lick the stamps and envelopes. We used a typewriter, resume-quality paper, envelopes, handwriting (cursive!), lickable stamps, and a post office.

Those days are LONG gone!

Job hunting today has turned digital practically overnight and nearly every job requires an online application. The process may seem easier until you get deep into the process and realize, after applying to hundreds of jobs, that you aren't getting any interviews. Why?

One potential culprit: ATS.

ATS stands for "applicant tracking system" and involves software designed to simplify the process of finding qualified candidates for recruiters. It didn't take long for recruiters and hiring managers to become bombarded with hundreds of applications each day for any one job. Additionally, the larger the company (such as IBM, Google, Amazon), the more quickly those applications can add up to thousands. The solution came in the form of ATS.

Good for recruiters. Not so good for applicants. Why?

Because few job seekers know of its existence.

What does ATS do? The artificial intelligence built into the ATS software screens and reviews every resume submitted. Each resume is scored against the keywords within the job description. Applications that score above 80% advance to the recruiter's desk; the remaining applications are rejected. Without that high score, your opportunity to reach a human recruiter or an interview is lost instantaneously!

First please the computer, then please the recruiter.

To beat ATS, you must think like the software. That means abandoning the eye-catching, colorful resumes that were popular in the past. ATS works in tandem with OCR—Optical Character Recognition—to scan your file, convert it into a plain text format, then extract your information and experiences from that file. Fancy fonts, blocks, boxes, tables, or other eye-appealing designs will only confuse ATS, and result in an immediate rejection. To increase your score and reach a human recruiter, these nine points will help you beat ATS.

Top Nine Actions to Optimize Your Resume for ATS

1. Choose the right font. Acceptable font styles are sans serif, i.e., Arial, Calibri, Helvetica. Once you've chosen, stick with this font throughout. You can use bold, small caps, all caps, etc., for emphasis, but keep the font style the same.

2. Set standard margins. ATS reads up and down the page, not left to right, so be sure to left-justify all page content, including bulleted items. The hard-and-fast rule of 1" margins no longer holds. A margin of 0.5" all around works just fine.

3. Avoid tables, cells, graphs, boxes, or columns. ATS cannot read these features. When using bullet points, only use the "dot" (•) as ATS cannot read other bullet styles.

4. Avoid use of headers and footers. Do not put contact information or page numbers in headers and footers. ATS cannot read these areas of the page.

5. Include your LinkedIn profile link with your contact information. Many studies have shown that the profile link is equally, if not more, important than your geographical information. Do not add your personal street address—only city, state, and zip code.

6. Front-load your resume. Place your most important qualifications, skills, and keywords on the first page. Busy recruiters review a resume's first page more thoroughly than ensuing pages and are far more interested in your most current skills.

7. Tailor your resume for each job to which you apply. This is critical as every job link (i.e., job opening) does not use the same keywords. It can be tedious and frustrating, but the process will get you into the hands of a human recruiter. As a test, Public ATS systems, such as SkillSyncer, allow you to copy/paste your resume and a job description, which is then scanned and scored. You'll know instantly if your resume will pass ATS.

8. Watch those acronyms. If you earned a degree in Engineering, write it out: Bachelor of Science (BS) in Engineering. ATS cannot understand acronyms, so always spell them out and place acronyms in parentheses to ensure you get credit for your accomplishments. For degrees that you would typically list at the end of your name, skip these in your contact information area and mention them elsewhere in the document. NOTE: Adding acronyms to the end of your name can cause ATS to assume those letters are part of your last name, which can cause a host of issues in terms of identifying you, filing your resume for the future, etc. Whenever

possible, spell out degree names, followed by the commonly used acronyms, e.g., Master of Social Work (MSW) or Human Resources (HR).

9. Spell check! Nothing kills your chances of an interview faster than spelling, grammar, and punctuation mistakes. Ask a friend to help or use an app like Grammarly to do a more thorough check than can be done with Word's version of spell check.

Adapted with permission from "Job Hunting Tips to Beat ATS and Ageism," by Kristen Edens, April 19, 2020, Managing Midlife at https://kristenedens.com/job-hunting-tips-to-beat-ats-and-ageism/

Budget Your Time Effectively

In order to maximize your productivity during a job search, you'll want to approach the process as if it's your actual job. Key elements to include in your weekly schedule are

- Search for new jobs or positions (long-term and short-term)
- Research companies and positions
- Request referrals from family, friends, colleagues, and online connections
- Customize resumes and cover letters for each position
- Submit job applications
- Follow up on applications if no response within two weeks
- Network with people in both your professional community and circle of family, friends, and acquaintances who may be able to help you make connections
- Learn new skills (e.g., Spanish, WordPress, project management)
- Volunteer to gain additional experience depending on positions you want to pursue
- Eat a healthy breakfast, lunch, and dinner daily
- Take three-to-four stretch breaks per day
- Practice self-care
- Balance your schedule with the needs of your family, if applicable

Here are three different approaches to building a weekly schedule depending on the extent to which you prefer to

(1) Compartmentalize tasks

(2) Complete the entire, step-by-step process daily

(3) Operate with maximum flexibility

Approach #1: Compartmentalize Tasks

Directions: Each day, focus exclusively on *one or two tasks* from the list on the previous page, taking care to eat three healthy meals, get up and stretch three or four times, practice self-care, and consider the needs of your family. For example,

Monday	• Spend the day searching for 6-8 excellent jobs or positions
Tuesday	• Research these 6-8 positions and their companies • Participate in a Zoom networking event
Wednesday	• Request 3 referrals • Customize resumes and cover letters for these 6–8 jobs
Thursday	• Submit these 6–8 job applications • Network with a friend or colleague via FaceTime or Skype
Friday	• Follow up on applications if no response within two weeks • Volunteer and/or learn new skills (2 hrs. Spanish)

Approach #2: Complete the Entire, Step-by-Step Process Daily

Directions: Build into your daily schedule *every task* associated with the job search process, interspersing networking and learning events throughout the week. Again, remember to eat three healthy meals, stretch 3–4 times per day, practice self-care, and include family time in your schedule as needed. Doing so will allow you to clear your mind, flex your body, refresh your spirit, and take care of your family. For example,

Monday	**Morning:**
	• Search for 1–2 new jobs or positions
	• Research these 1–2 positions and their companies
	• Request 1 referral
	Afternoon:
	• Customize resumes/cover letters for these 1–2 positions
	• Submit these 1–2 job applications
	• Follow up on applications
Tuesday	• Repeat Monday schedule
	• Participate in a Zoom networking event
Wednesday	• Repeat Monday schedule
	• Request 1 referral
Thursday	• Repeat Monday schedule
	• Network with a friend or colleague via FaceTime or Skype
	• Request 1 referral
Friday	• Repeat Monday schedule
	• Learn new skills (2 hrs. Spanish)
	• Volunteer

Approach #3: Maximize Flexibility, but Get the Job Done

Directions: Instead of setting daily goals, establish *weekly goals* that allow you to complete all tasks with maximum flexibility. Again, distribute networking and learning events throughout the week. You know the daily drill: three healthy meals, three or four stretch breaks, self-care, and family time as needed. For example,

Week #1
- Spend a couple of hours each day searching for job openings
- Identify 6–8 great companies to apply for this week
- Research companies and positions
- Request 3 referrals
- Customize resumes and cover letters for each position
- Submit applications
- Follow-up on applications
- Participate in at least 2 networking events
- Learn new skills (2 hrs. Spanish)
- Volunteer

Which of the three approaches appeals most to you?

☐ Compartmentalize tasks in blocks of quality time
☐ Complete the entire, step-by-step process daily
☐ Maximize flexibility, but get the job done

Why do you prefer this approach?

_____

_____

_____

_____

_____

In the exercise on the following page, we'll take some time to build your "ideal daily schedule" around your preferred approach to see how well the two might work in tandem for you.

Create Your Ideal Daily Schedule

Creating an effective, *sustainable* job search requires designing and executing a game plan that helps you to minimize stress and burnout, particularly in times of increased pressure and anxiety. What would an ideal day look like if you treated your job search as your "real job"—a job to which you could look forward to going on a regular basis? How many hours per day would you work? What time would you start and end your workday? How much time would you allot for breaks and healthy meals? Would you build in time for exercise? Use the space on the following page to map out your ideal daily schedule based on the approach you liked most in the previous exercise. Don't worry about getting the timing perfect. That's the beauty of a daily calendar. You can revise and adjust as you go.

Here's a sample schedule using Approach #2 from the previous exercise:

6:45 a.m.	Rise and shine. Shower and dress for the day. Eat a good breakfast. (75 mins)
8:00 a.m.	Search for jobs. Identify top 2 positions. (75 mins)
9:15 a.m.	Take a stretch break. Go outside and play fetch with the dog. (15 mins)
9:30 a.m.	Conduct web research on companies advertising top 2 positions. (75 mins)
10:45 a.m.	Step outside and take several deep breaths. Top off bird feeders. (15 mins)
11:00 a.m.	Customize resumes and cover letters for top 2 positions. (75 mins)
12:15 p.m.	Yay, lunchtime! (45 mins)
1:00 p.m.	Continue customizing resumes/cover letters for top 2 positions. (75 mins)
2:15 p.m.	Go for a 3-mile run. (60 mins)
3:15 p.m.	Submit 2 applications. Network via email and LinkedIn. (75 mins)
4:30 p.m.	Call it a good day

Please note! Assuming that you're responsible for childcare during the day, you can easily adapt this schedule as needed.

It's your turn. What would your ideal daily schedule look like? Use the space on the following page to map out your optimal schedule.

My Ideal Daily Schedule

Start Time   Tasks

_____   _____

_____   _____

_____   _____

_____   _____

_____   _____

_____   _____

_____   _____

_____   _____

_____   _____

_____   _____

_____   _____

Once you've drafted an initial schedule, give it a test drive. Determine what works well and not-so-well. Then, modify your proposed plan based on what you've learned, and try out your revision. Repeat the process until you have developed an ideal schedule that works for you. Then, make multiple copies for your daily use.

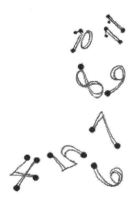

How to Stay Productive During Your Job Search

How many times have you sabotaged your success by setting unrealistic goals? It may have been that New Year's resolution to completely change your eating habits or to adopt a rigorous exercise program when you've thoroughly enjoyed life as a "couch potato" for the past two years.

In the same way, we can set unrealistic goals for ourselves during a job or career change, which can make the process even more dreadful and daunting. For example, consider the following simple, well-meaning goal:

"Every week, I'm going to send out 5–7 resumes daily on Monday – Friday."

Now consider the reality of following through on this goal.

In order to send out 5–7 resumes *daily* (quick math: that means 25–35 resumes weekly), you're first going to have to identify 25–35 open positions that you would like to pursue...every single week of your job search. What are the chances you're going to find that many great job openings every week? More importantly, what will happen to your energy and engagement levels the first week that you fail to achieve this goal? Not pretty.

Rather than setting such "hard and fast" goals, why not come up with Plan A, Plan B, and Plan C for each week using the following parameters:

Plan A: Completely and totally acceptable week (Good job!)
Plan B: Great week—Actually surprised myself (Even better)
Plan C: I'm a world-class, job-search guru (Personal best)

Please note: Plan A is not defined as minimally acceptable, but instead as COMPLETELY and TOTALLY acceptable. You'll be amazed at the difference in mindset that results when you reframe Plan A in this way. And you can be proud of your accomplishments.

Each week, begin by identifying your Plans A, B, and C. Then choose the plan you want to attempt and see how well it works for you.

By starting each week with three possible plans, you can quickly adapt the plan that you're using mid-week, depending on your situation and what you've learned about yourself.

Following is an example using Approach #3 presented in the *Budget Your Time Effectively* exercise.

Week #1: Plans A, B, and C

Plan A: Completely and Totally Acceptable Week (Good job!)
- Spend 1–2 hours per day searching for job openings
- Identify 4–5 great positions to apply for this week
- Research companies and positions
- Request 1 referral
- Customize resumes/cover letters for each position
- Submit applications; follow up on applications
- Participate in 1 online networking event
- Practice my Spanish 1–2 hours this week
- Eat 3 healthy meals; take 3–4 stretch breaks daily
- Exercise 3 times this week
- Family responsibilities (if applicable)

Plan B: Great Week—Actually Surprised Myself (Even Better)
- Spend 2–3 hours per day searching for job openings
- Identify 5–7 great positions to apply for this week
- Research companies and positions
- Request 2 referrals
- Customize resumes/cover letters for each position
- Submit applications; follow up on applications
- Actively engage in 2 online networking events
- Study Spanish 2–3 hours this week
- Eat 3 healthy meals; take 3–4 stretch breaks daily
- Exercise 4 times this week
- Family responsibilities (if applicable)

Plan C: I'm a World-Class, Job-Search Guru (Personal Best)
- Spend 2–3 hours per day searching for job openings
- Identify 6–8 great positions to apply for this week
- Research companies and positions
- Request 3 referrals
- Customize resumes/cover letters for each position
- Submit applications; follow-up on applications
- Participate in 2 networking events; host an online event
- Study Spanish 4 hours this week

- Volunteer with a youth group once this week
- Eat 3 healthy meals; take 3–4 stretch breaks daily
- Exercise 4 times this week
- Family responsibilities (if applicable)

It's your turn. Give it a go. We'll check in after you've completed the exercise.

Week # _____

Plan A: Completely and Totally Acceptable Week (Good Job!)

_____

_____

_____

_____

_____

_____

_____

_____

Plan B: Great Week—Actually Surprised Myself (Even Better)

_____

_____

_____

_____

_____

_____

_____

Plan C: I'm a World-Class, Job-Search Guru (Personal Best)

_____

_____

_____

_____

_____

_____

_____

_____

How do each of these three plans feel to you? To what extent have you included the right amount of increasing challenge?

What happens to your energy level when you think about each plan? Given the energy level that you associate with each plan, which one would you like to begin your job search with next week?

What will you do during the week if you start to see your plan failing to materialize? How can you adapt your plan in such a way that the outcome is COMPLETELY and TOTALLY Acceptable?

Keep Up with Your Job Applications

When we experience elevated levels of anxiety and stress, it's perfectly normal to feel absent minded and scatterbrained. According to Corinne Purtill, "Stress, like a pandemic, puts our brains into "fight or flight" mode, disrupting attention, memory, breathing and sleep....Chronic stress can also cause fatigue, problems concentrating, irritability, and changes in sleep and appetite."[23]

One way to address the problem as it relates to staying on top of your job search is to diligently keep track of your job applications and their status, either electronically or using a three-ring binder. We recommend implementing an easy, two-step process that offers you (1) a quick glance at the status of your applications across the board, and (2) a more detailed log for each application, where you can capture notes at every step.

To develop your own *Quick View Log*, create a print binder, Excel spreadsheet, or table in Word (or your favorite word-processing program). As soon as you submit a job application, input the following information into your paper or electronic file: date job found, date applied, company name, position/job title, how application was sent, version of resume sent, version of cover letter sent, and source of job lead or referral.

As soon as each job application moves forward in the process, create a *Detailed Job-Search Log* for the specific job or position, again in print or electronic form. Doing so will help you to stay on top of your job search, ensure that nothing falls between the cracks, and allow you to play at the top of your game. (In the process, you'll also be managing stress.)

In the following pages, you will find templates for a Quick View Log and Detailed Job-Search Log as well as a *Company Information* form. Feel free to use, adapt, and share these templates with others. We've designed them for your use.

Job Applications Quick View

Date Job Found	Date Applied	Company Name	Position/ Job Title	How Application Was Sent (e.g., Email, LinkedIn)	Version of Resume Sent	Version of Cover Letter Sent	Source of Job Lead or Referral

Detailed Job-Search Log

Date Job Found: —————————   Date Applied: ——————————

Company Name: ————————————————————

Position/Job Title: ————————————————————

Source of Job Lead: ————————————————————

Referral (if any): ————————————————————

Recruiter Name and Contact Information: ————————————

————————————————————————————

Version of Resume Sent: ————————————

Version of Cover Letter Sent: ————————————

How Application Was Sent: ————————————————

Follow-up Notes: ————————————————————

————————————————————————————

————————————————————————————

————————————————————————————

————————————————————————————

Outcome: ————————————————————————

Interview #1:   Date: ——————————   Time: ——————————

Type of Interview (circle)   Informational   Screening   Selection/Hiring

Interviewer Names and Titles:

————————————————————————————

————————————————————————————

————————————————————————————

Interview Location:

_____

_____

Interview Notes:

_____

_____

_____

_____

_____

_____

_____

_____

_____

Interview #2:   Date: _____ Time: _____

Type of Interview (circle)   Screening   Selection/Hiring

Interviewer Names and Titles:

_____

_____

_____

_____

Interview Location:

_____

_____

Interview Notes:

_____

_____

_____

_____

_____

_____

_____

Interview #3:   Date: _____ Time: _____

Type of Interview (circle)   Screening   Selection/Hiring

Interviewer Names and Titles:

_____

_____

_____

_____

Interview Location:

_____

Interview Notes:

_____

_____

_____

_____

_____

_____

_____

Company Information

Company Name: —————————————

Recruiter Name: —————————————

Phone: ————————————— Email Address: —————————————

Physical Address:

_____

_____

Information About Position/Job:

_____

_____

_____

_____

_____

_____

_____

_____

_____

_____

Source(s) of Information:

_____

_____

_____

_____

_____

Information about Company:

_____

_____

_____

_____

_____

_____

_____

_____

Source(s) of Information:

_____

_____

_____

_____

_____

Aha Moments

A Different Take on Job Interviews

"You will never be more powerful than the moment before you accept a job. You will never be less powerful than the moment after you sign on the dotted line."

— Anonymous

So much great advice is available online about preparing for job interviews in difficult times. In fact, a quick Google search nets a plethora of entries if you type in the following two searches: "preparing for job interviews AND economic downturns" and "preparing for job interviews AND pandemic."

Far less has been written about the value of approaching an interview as a two-way street, a level playing field, and an opportunity to ask hard questions that ensure the company and position are right for YOU.

When you get to that point in an interview when the interviewer invites you to ask questions, it's your turn to shine. The more thoughtful and well-conceived your questions are, the more impressed your interviewer will be. In fact, if your interviewer fails to take an active interest in your questions, you may want to re-think working for his or her company.

Not convinced? Imagine yourself in the role of an interviewer for a position with your own company. You are interviewing a smart, engaging prospect, and you are impressed with her background and experience. You've just spent 30 minutes asking tough, compelling questions designed to see if she can make the cut. With 15 minutes remaining, you ask the recruit if she has any questions, expecting little more than standard, "softball" questions. Instead, your prospect respectfully replies, "Actually, I have a few questions. Would you mind if I take notes?" She proceeds to ask 3–5 powerful, thought-provoking questions that clearly will determine if your company will make the cut with HER. As the original interviewer in this scenario, how would you feel and respond? Would you sit up a little straighter in your chair, stop thinking about the next thing on your To Do List, and pay closer attention? Would you think more highly of the recruit for having the courage and confidence to ask YOU tough questions?

Several great questions that you could ask a potential employer are

1. What do you like most and least about working for Company X?
2. What specific qualities or traits are you looking for in the person whom you would like to hire?
3. What are the greatest challenges that your new hire will face in this position?
4. What would an average "day in the life" look like for this person at work?

5. What professional-development and promotion opportunities will be available for your new hire?
6. Please tell me about the supervisor who is overseeing this position. What are his or her greatest strengths and opportunities for growth as a manager?
7. What advice would you offer to the person who ultimately accepts this job?

AVOID asking questions about salary, benefits, and perks (e.g., raises, insurance programs, vacation days, etc.) until you are discussing an actual offer. In fact, here is a link to a great article that discusses *45 bad questions* to ask:

https://www.job-hunt.org/job_interviews/avoid-asking-bad-questions.shtml

Again, we recommend asking no more than 3–5 questions during an interview until you have received a viable job offer.

Consider capturing your interview notes in the Detailed Job-Search Log.

How would you feel about going into an interview if you believed the process is truly a two-way street?

Imagine YOURSELF asking interview questions like the ones we've recommended. How would you feel? What are the benefits of *asking* such questions? *Of getting answers* to these questions?

What other interview questions could you ask that would help you make a good decision about your next career move?

Adopting this approach to interviews requires courage, grace, and confidence. The keys to success when "accepting the reins" of an interview are

- Practice, practice, practice asking tough interview questions with friends and colleagues until you feel confident doing so.
- Let the interviewer know the number of questions you plan to ask and stick to these questions. End. Period. Stop.
- Request permission to take notes before asking questions.
- Frame the wording of each question in a positive way. (E.g., Rather than inquiring about a supervisor's "weaknesses," ask about his or her "strengths and opportunities for growth.")
- Ask questions confidently, but respectfully. Avoid coming across as either
  - boastful, cocky, and arrogant
  - shy and apologetic
- Maintain a gracious, thoughtful demeanor with your gestures, facial expressions, and eye contact.
- Sit up straight without allowing your posture to appear tense or rigid. You don't have to feel confident to look confident.
- Show sincere interest and appreciation for the other person's responses.
- Once you've asked your final question, genuinely thank the interviewer without exhibiting fawning or effusive behavior.
- Maintain eye contact with the interviewer (or camera lens) until the end of the session.

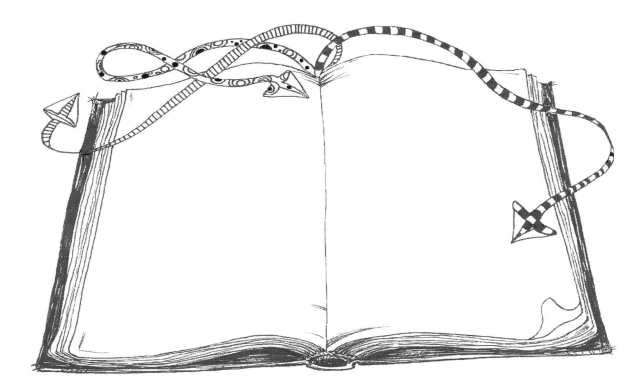

Interview to Vet Your Next Boss

Most of us would do almost anything to avoid a terrible boss. However, once we've accepted a job, we can find ourselves with little or no control over the situation. One way to get ahead of the curve ball is to leverage the interview process for critical information about potential managers and supervisors. Work/life expert Monica Torres recommends asking one or two interview questions based on the experiences that we're trying to avoid. For example, if you want to avoid a disengaged boss, ask how often he or she checks in with the team. If you want to avoid a boss who is a poor communicator, ask how often his or her people receive feedback about their work.[24]

Below are five categories of behavior that you may want to consider when constructing such interview questions. For each category, list at least two good interview questions that you could ask to assess the potential fit between you and your potential boss.

1. Interpersonal communication style (passive, aggressive, passive-aggressive, assertive)

   Example: *I would love to learn more about the supervisor for this position. How is he or she staying in touch with employees who are working remotely?*

   • _____

   _____

   _____

   • _____

   _____

   _____

2. Leadership style (autocratic, bureaucratic, charismatic, democratic, laissez-faire, servant, transactional, transformational)

   Example: *How would you describe the leadership style of the supervisor in times of crisis?*

   • _____

   _____

   _____

- _____

  _____

  _____

3. Approach to motivation (employs *extrinsic* motivators – incentives, fear, power, affiliation; uses *intrinsic* motivators – competence/learning, attitudes, achievement, creativity)

   Example: *What three words would you use to describe the supervisor's approach to motivating his or her employees?*

   - _____

     _____

     _____

   - _____

     _____

     _____

4. Approach to decision-making and problem-solving (top-down, bottom-up, collaborative)

   Example: *How does the supervisor make decisions or solve problems affecting the team?*

   - _____

     _____

     _____

   - _____

     _____

     _____

5. Conflict management style (avoiding, accommodating, competing, compromising, collaborating)

   Example: *To what extent does the supervisor leverage collaboration to manage team conflict?*

   - _____

     _____

     _____

     _____

   - _____

     _____

     _____

     _____

   What other questions would you like to ask about your potential supervisor or manager if you could frame the questions thoughtfully and diplomatically?

Torres recommends that you "save deeper management style questions until you are in the final stages of an interview, and know you want the job."[25] Additionally, she suggests that you be on the lookout for (a) evasive answers, (b) people whom the interviewer credits for success (themselves, managers, supervisors, or the team), and (c) tone of voice (e.g., defensive, irritated, warm, and open).

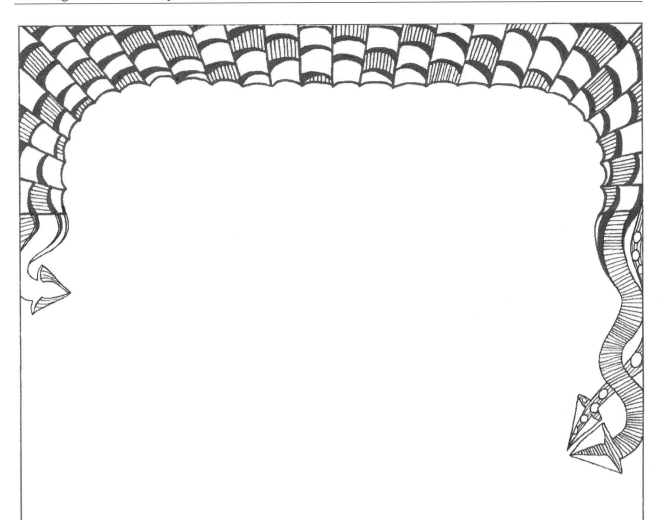

Random Thoughts

Networking in This Crazy Online World

For many, the mere thought of networking can quickly rattle our nerves. Add to the mix the perils of economic upheaval or other traumatic life events, and the idea of networking can be nothing short of mind boggling.

However, networking doesn't have to be scary if we remember its purpose: to develop authentic relationships with people who can help us to (1) identify opportunities for collaboration, (2) increase visibility in our respective fields, (3) keep abreast of industry developments, (4) discover hidden job openings, and (5) connect with the right people in companies in which we're interested.[26] However, to create a powerful network, it's crucial to remember that networking is a two-way street. We must be committed to offering the same benefits to others.

To help you develop a robust network of connections that can support you through a serious job search and beyond, let's explore three major topics: (1) steps you can take to grow your network; (2) technologies you can leverage to connect with people without meeting face-to-face; and (3) creative ways you can stay "social" from home if necessary.

Four Steps to Grow Your Network

The first step in growing your network is to identify the people whom you consider to be your *current connections*. To do so, simply create (or update) a list of personal and professional contacts that you have at this moment—people to whom you can easily reach out for advice and guidance. Include friends, neighbors, relatives, bosses, colleagues, and meaningful connections that you have made on social media.

Your file can take the form of a Word document, Excel spreadsheet, or physical rolodex. For each contact, include the person's

Name: _____ Job Title: _____

Type of Connection: _____ Personal _____ Professional

Company Name: _____

Phone: _____ Email: _____

His or Her Preferred Social Media:

_____ LinkedIn   _____ Instagram   _____ YouTube

_____ Facebook   _____ Twitter   _____ Other

Ways This Person Has Supported You in the Past:

_____

_____

_____

_____

Ways You Could Return the Favor:

_____

_____

_____

_____

Second, brainstorm *past connections* that you could revive in order to share possible leads, professional recommendations, and job opportunities. Include former bosses and colleagues; old classmates and friends; and previous neighbors.[27] Brainstorm your list of possible contacts in the space below:

Then, convert your brainstorming session into the list of *past connections* with whom you would like to reconnect, and track down their contact information. Set a deadline to reach out to each person in the next two weeks. (Note: If you're an introvert and reluctant to make these kinds of contacts, ask a family member, friend, or colleague to help.) Before making contact, consider the request you will make (e.g., advice and guidance about a company or industry; LinkedIn endorsement; referral; etc.) and ways you can return the favor. If all goes well with the call, then add your past connection's name and pertinent information to your file of current connections. Feel free to use the following space to capture information about your past connections.

Name	Contact Information	Date I Will Make Contact	Past Connections	
			Request I Will Make	Ways I Can Return the Favor

Third, consider *new connections* that have the potential to be meaningful, authentic, and mutually beneficial. Include people whom you would like to know; members of professional associations with which you're affiliated; people affiliated with high school, college, or university alumni groups; and second-degree connections on LinkedIn.[28] Take a big gulp and brainstorm their names here:

Again, turn your brainstorming session into a list of *new connections* that you will commit to making in the next two weeks. Assign a specific date when you'll make initial contact or ask someone to help you reach out. Consider requests you could make of them and ways to return the favor. If you share a meaningful conversation, then add the person's name and pertinent information to your file of current connections. Again, feel free to use the following page to capture information regarding your new connections.

New Connections

Name	Contact Information	Date I Will Make Contact	Request I Will Make	Ways I Can Return the Favor

Fourth, explore industry associations and professional groups that you can join to grow your network. Many are now offering opportunities to network online via "Zoom meetings," webinars, and live Facebook sessions. Additionally, hundreds of professional groups exist on LinkedIn, with which you can easily connect. To conduct a LinkedIn search, key into the search bar the types of groups in which you're interested (e.g., "recruitment groups," "coach groups," "engineer groups," etc.) You will be amazed at the wide variety of groups that are regularly getting together online.[29]

Once you've spent time checking out the opportunities, use the space below to capture the names of 5–7 groups that you would be interested in pursuing.

1. _____
2. _____
3. _____
4. _____
5. _____
6. _____
7. _____

As you steadily build your network, keep a running list of companies for which you would like to work or that have positions for which you would like to apply. Then, identify people in your network who may be able to help you learn more or make connections inside those companies. As before, be prepared by understanding the request you will make and ways you can return the favor. Use the following space (or create a spreadsheet) to capture this information, including specific dates when you plan to make contact.

Company or Position of Interest	Name of Person I Can Contact	Date I Will Reach Out	My Connections	
			Request I Will Make	Ways I Can Return the Favor

Most importantly, remember to thank people who contribute to your job-search success. Although an email or phone call is acceptable, a handwritten thank-you note is still the ultimate way to say, "Thank You."

Technologies You Can Use to Network

When we think about networking, we most often think of face-to-face events. However, the times in which we're living are causing us to re-think old ways of doing things, including the ways that we use technology.

Each of the following are excellent ways to connect with people without meeting face-to-face. Place an X in the box (or the circle) beside each of the ways with which you are currently comfortable interacting with people. Then, circle at least two new networking methods that you are willing to try in the next 7–10 days.

- ☐ Telephone
    - o Audio only
    - o Audio/video (e.g., Skype, Facetime)
- ☐ Text or instant messaging
- ☐ Social media – six best platforms for business[30]
    - o Facebook
    - o Twitter
    - o Instagram
    - o Pinterest
    - o LinkedIn
    - o YouTube
- ☐ Online meetings (e.g., Zoom, UberConference, Cisco WebEx)
- ☐ Online forums/posting sites
- ☐ Webinars

What do you like most and least about networking with the methods you're currently comfortable with?

_____

_____

_____

What would it take to get you to test drive the new networking methods you circled?

_____

_____

_____

Creative Ways to Stay "Social" from Home

Below are 11 creative ways to stay social from home if you're unable to meet face-to-face with other people. Place a ✔ in the box beside each of the ways you would be willing to try in the next week to grow and nurture your network.

- ☐ Invite a colleague to meet for virtual coffee
- ☐ Launch a Twitter account to build your professional brand
- ☐ Conduct a 15-minute informational interview with someone whom you would like to meet and write a LinkedIn post or article about the person or interview (Note: Doing so can help you build credibility and generate engagement.)
- ☐ Ask a friend to conduct a practice interview with you via Skype, Zoom, or UberConference
- ☐ Host a virtual happy hour (maximum: 2 glasses of wine!)
- ☐ Volunteer from home (e.g., participate in a fund-raising event or launch a movement)
- ☐ Take turns partnering with a friend or colleague to teach new skills
- ☐ Join a weekly, virtual Meet-up group
- ☐ Meet for a lunch date on Google Meet
- ☐ Connect via a Facebook or LinkedIn group to discuss mutual interests
- ☐ Teach new skills to the world via YouTube[31,32]

As you can see, networking is all about connecting with others and finding ways to help each other to

- learn and grow as human beings
- move forward in our lives and careers
- achieve our goals, missions, and dreams

What makes networking different today is the extent to which we're learning to be creative with technology to accomplish these objectives.

Don't be afraid to try new things as you develop your networking skills.

The key to success is practicing new technologies with family and friends before attempting them with professional colleagues.

Doing so not only will increase your confidence using these new technologies, but also allow you to focus on what is most important: making meaningful, authentic, and rewarding connections.

Maintain Bridges to Meaningful and Important Relationships

Any time we change jobs—by necessity or choice—we risk losing valued and valuable relationships, including those with managers, supervisors, employees, mentors, colleagues, and friends. The situation can even damage relationships with family members, depending on the circumstances of our departures and risks to the safety and well-being of our families.

If you're furloughed, laid off, or fired from your position, you may feel angry, fearful, and hurt. If you've lost a small business, you also may feel hopeless and devastated. These feelings are *completely understandable*, and you will need time to grieve and process your loss. If you're leaving your job situation by choice, you may feel elated, relieved, and excited, which also is natural and normal. In any case, you may be tempted to sever all ties with the past in order to make a fresh start. However, we strongly discourage you from "burning bridges" in the heat of the moment. You will want to leave your situation with courage, grace, and no regrets – knowing that you made a difference with the time you had.

To help you honor and protect your most valued work relationships, we encourage you to complete the following exercise.

Identify the top 5–7 people at your previous (or current) job whose friendships you most value.

1.

2.

3.

4.

5.

6.

7.

For each person on the list, how could the two of you assist one another in the future, from sharing advice and guidance to making introductions to important people in your respective networks?

Top 5–7 Valued Contacts	Ways We Could Assist Each Other Going Forward
1.	
2.	
3.	
4.	
5.	
6.	
7.	

If possible, make every effort to secure each person's contact information before your last day with the company. You can capture that information here:

Name	Telephone Number	Email Address
1.		
2.		
3.		
4.		
5.		
6.		
7.		

What are the best and worst possible outcomes that could result if you (a) made contact with each person right now, (b) shared how much you value the relationship, and (c) asked for assistance with your job search?

Name	Best Possible Outcome	Worst Possible Outcome
1.		
2.		
3.		
4.		
5.		
6.		
7.		

As with all effective interpersonal communication, both WHAT you say and HOW you say it make all the difference in maintaining bridges to meaningful and important relationships.

Use the following space to brainstorm elements of a simple email message that you could send whose purpose would be to honor and protect your valued relationship in the face of your job or career change:

How committed are you to reaching out to your top 5–7 connections to ensure continued, mutual growth and development? (1 = Low; 10 = High)

1   2   3   4   5   6   7   8   9   10

If your commitment score above is less than 8, what would it take to increase your commitment level by one or two steps?

By what date in the coming days or weeks are you committed to contacting your top 5-7 people?

Name	Date
1.	
2.	
3.	
4.	
5.	
6.	
7.	

Seek Support from Your Family

The process of changing, losing, or seeking a new job or career can involve an inordinate amount of risk, uncertainty, and vulnerability for everyone involved. If your spouse, life partner, or children are directly impacted, then it's important for you to seek their input and support from the outset. Doing so will help you and your family to

- Keep the lines of communication open
- Reduce potential conflict in your relationship
- Make decisions and solve problems more effectively as a team
- Share much-needed encouragement and support
- Manage uncertainty throughout the process

This guidance is especially true for spouses or partners who have different risk-tolerance levels related to money and financial security. If you personally have a high tolerance for risk and are willing to take a financial gamble, you may be willing to dip into savings or retirement accounts to support your family throughout the process. However, if your life partner has a lower tolerance for financial risk than you, then you can see the problems that could quickly emerge.

If you're currently in a committed relationship, how would you rate both your and your partner's current financial-risk tolerance levels? (1=Very Low; 10=Very High)

My own financial-risk tolerance score:

Very Low									Very High
1	2	3	4	5	6	7	8	9	10

My score for my partner:

Very Low									Very High
1	2	3	4	5	6	7	8	9	10

Subtract the lower score from the higher score to calculate the difference in your perceived risk-tolerance levels. For example, if you gave yourself a score of 9 and your partner a score of 7, then the difference would be 2 steps apart.

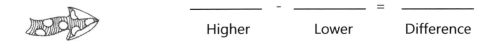

_____ - _____ = _____

    Higher   Lower   Difference

The closer your two scores are to one another, the less likely you will experience conflict in your relationship as you move forward with money decisions—assuming you communicate effectively about the subject. The greater the distance between the two scores, the greater the chance for conflict to arise.

To assess the accuracy of your scoring, ask your spouse or partner to complete the same exercise (on the following page). You may be surprised by the scores he or she assigns. However, by bringing him or her into the discussion, you will achieve a more realistic view of the situation and open the dialogue about money issues as you transition to your new job or career.

Record your partner's scores in the space below.

<u>My partner's own financial-risk tolerance score:</u>

Very Low									Very High
1	2	3	4	5	6	7	8	9	10

<u>My partner's score for me:</u>

Very Low									Very High
1	2	3	4	5	6	7	8	9	10

Again, subtract the lower score from the higher score to calculate the difference.

_____ - _____ = _____

Higher   Lower   Difference

So, how did it go? How closely did your scoring align?

_____

_____

_____

_____

What did you learn about yourself, your partner, and your situation from completing this exercise?

_____

_____

_____

_____

_____

In light of the discussion, how can the two of you approach your day-to-day finances in such a way to effectively address your respective risk-tolerance needs? What are the ramifications of this exercise for the salary you need to earn in your next position?

_____

_____

_____

_____

_____

_____

How could you use this learning to open the doors to more effective communication about money with your life partner?

_____

_____

_____

_____

_____

_____

What specific communication plan could you put into place to regularly check in and keep the lines of communication open with your spouse or partner throughout the job-change process?

_____

_____

_____

_____

_____

Communicating with Children and Others
Living in Your Household

Given that your job or career change will affect the lives of your kids and others living in your household, you will want to have a well-conceived game plan for communicating with them before, during, and after your job search.

According to Elizabeth Alterman, your primary aims with *children* are to (a) provide stability and reassurance; (b) establish the importance of working together as a team; and (c) address their fears calmly and openly.[33]

If you have children, the details of your plan will differ depending on their ages and the need to be age appropriate.

What expectations will you have of your children? (E.g., "Doing as they are told" the first time a request is made; sharing household duties and responsibilities; helping one another to get things done; allowing you quiet time while you work.)

What expectations can your children have of you? (E.g., Meeting their safety and security needs—for example, food, clothing, a safe place to live; offering them physical, mental, and emotional support; committing to a certain amount of quality time to be spent with them each day or week.)

Given the three aims articulated by Alterman on the prior page, what is your plan for communicating with each of your children if this question applies? Here is some space where you can brainstorm:

Likewise, take time to communicate your needs, plans, goals, and expectations with *others who may share your home* (e.g., aging parents, young grandchildren, roommates, etc.). Doing so will go a long way toward helping you "keep the peace" and maximize success with your job search. Here is some space you can use to make a few notes about communicating with them:

What's Holding You Back?

Job or career changes can be exciting, exasperating, thrilling, exhausting, and fraught with peril—both real and imagined. Wherever you are in the process, stop for a moment and consider the things that are holding you back from moving confidently toward your future. Try to be thorough and complete as you consider your roadblocks. Here are three examples:

A. Need to find a job quickly to support my family and pay the bills before we run out of money
B. Unable to overcome my fear and anxiety long enough to stay focused on the job search
C. Lack of success securing an initial interview despite having submitted more than 80 job applications

What roadblocks are holding you back? Use the following space to brainstorm your response.

Now that you have generated an overall list of roadblocks, identify your top three in rank order, with #1 being your most troublesome roadblock.

1. _____

_____

_____

2. _____

_____

_____

3. _____

_____

_____

Next, let's brainstorm specific ways to go over, under, around, or through each of these three roadblocks.

Here are two sample brainstorming sessions associated with Examples A and B above:

A. Need to find a job quickly to support my family and pay the bills before we run out of money

- Create a realistic monthly budget to confirm how much money we need to live
- Search simultaneously for short-term and long-term jobs to maximize potential to make money
- Explore the possibility of doing temporary, freelance, or contract work (e.g., part-time bookkeeping or accounting)
- Take on a "side hustle" selling (or reselling) products online
- Host a garage sale to downsize our household and get rid of unneeded stuff
- Consider renting a spare bedroom to a responsible college student

B. Unable to overcome my fear and anxiety long enough to stay focused on the job search

- Avoid isolating
- Practice presence in the moment
- Surround myself with positive people, and lose the pessimists, cynics, and naysayers
- Articulate a clear vision for myself; write it down; and access it regularly for motivation
- Set daily goals that are achievable and reward myself for accomplishments—large and small
- Schedule time for self-care: eat healthy meals, get 7–8 hours of sleep per night, hydrate throughout the day, and exercise regularly
- Speak with my doctor if my fear and anxiety become too debilitating
- Consider professional assistance if the problem is too great to handle alone

Now it's your turn. Use the space provided below to brainstorm solutions for each of the Top 3 Roadblocks that you identified on the prior pages.

Roadblock#1:

Roadblock #2:

Roadblock #3:

Half the battle of overcoming roadblocks during your job search is identifying and calling them out. Once you've articulated potential barriers, consider consulting a professional advisor or partnering with a trusted colleague or friend to brainstorm creative solutions. If you still find yourself feeling stuck, consider hiring a professional career coach to help you address your roadblocks. We can help.

Making Decisions Throughout Your Job Search

Throughout the process of changing jobs or careers, you will make a wide range of decisions—from the types of jobs you will pursue and people with whom you will network to the best ways to balance your job search with the needs of your family.

According to Christi Nix-Bloomer, Founder and CEO of In the Arena Coaching, you can optimize the decision-making process by leveraging Commitment, Accountability, Reason/Purpose, Mindset, and Action (CARMA):

- Commitment – How committed are you to doing what you have promised yourself to do? How would you rate your commitment level on a 1–10 scale? When you know that you need to earn a salary of $60,000 per year to live, do you crumble when you receive an offer of $55,000? If your commitment level regarding a decision is 4/10, what is one change you can make to create a stronger sense of necessity or make your decision more enticing?

- Accountability – Often decision-making fails to get us very far if we choose not to share our decisions with others. When you commit to waking up at 6 a.m. daily to start your job search, do you share your intention with others? Do you follow through and set an alarm? Do you assign yourself specific tasks to complete at 6 a.m.? Consider an accountability partner to help you do what you say you're going to do.

- Reason/Purpose – What is the reason you are here on this earth? What are your gifts—those that must be shared and make you special, different, and unique? What talent or skill do you have that you will die a slow death if you cannot share it with the world? THIS is your reason for being! Identify it, keep it close, and reflect on it often. It is your kick in the tail, the jolt to your soul.

- Mindset – Do you feel encouraged by a decision you are making, or does it feel like an obligation? (For example, does the idea of contacting a recruiter feel exciting or overwhelming?) If you accept the premise that our thoughts create our feelings and our feelings drive our actions, then decide how you WANT to think about something, and your feelings will follow.

- Action (A) – When we decide to do something (e.g., search for a job, attend a lunch-and-learn session, or start exercising again), we often wait until we feel motivated to do so. However, if we wait for inspiration to act, we will always be waiting. Try to remember why your decision is so important. Ask yourself what you need to think, feel, do, or say in order to remember your decision's relevance and value. Motivation often FOLLOWS action. Focus on moving first, and inspiration will follow.[34]

Hold Fast to Your Dreams

Section III

Start Where You Are

Sometimes identifying what you like most and least about your current work situation is a great place to begin if you're considering a new job or career. This is true no matter what kind of job, career, or situation you may be in at this moment.

Your Current Job Situation

If you're currently working, take into account the following as you work through this exercise: (1) future growth and development opportunities with your present company; (2) extent to which the work environment "brings out the best in you"; (3) your satisfaction with the organization's culture; and (4) the company's financial health—four major considerations according to *Forbes* magazine.[35] If you're not presently working, complete this exercise based on your most recent job or career experience.

What You Like Most and Least About Your Work

Likes	Dislikes

What You Like Most and Least About the People You Work With

Likes	Dislikes

What You Like Most and Least About Your Company or Organization

Pros	Cons

If you're having serious doubts about your career in general, generate a list of likes and dislikes in the space below.

What You Like Most and Least About Your Career

Pros	Cons

To what extent do your likes outweigh your dislikes about...?

- Your Work

- The People You Work With

- Your Company or Organization

- Your Career

What did you learn about yourself or your situation having completed this exercise?

Before jumping to any big conclusions, let's dig even deeper to see what else may be driving your quest for a new job or career.

How Well Do You and Your Company or Organization Make a Good Fit?

In the book *Fit Matters: How to Love Your Job*, Moe Carrick and Cammie Dunaway identified six elements of "work fit" that need to be aligned in order to feel that you and your company make a great fit:

1. <u>Meaning fit</u> – when you believe that the job you're doing is important
2. <u>Job fit</u> – when your talents line up with your roles and responsibilities, and you have growth and development opportunities
3. <u>Culture fit</u> – when your values and beliefs align with those of your company
4. <u>Relationship fit</u> – when you enjoy working with the people in your company and experience mutual trust and validation
5. <u>Lifestyle fit</u> – when your job fits well with the everyday life you want to lead
6. <u>Financial fit</u> – when you believe that you're receiving fair pay and benefits which adequately fulfill your needs[36]

When you think about your current or most recent job or career, how do you feel about the fit for each of these six elements? Capture your assessment in the space below using the following five-point rating scale: 1 = Very Poor, 2 = Poor, 3 = OK, 4 = Good, 5 = Very Good. Then, briefly explain why you rated each element as you did.

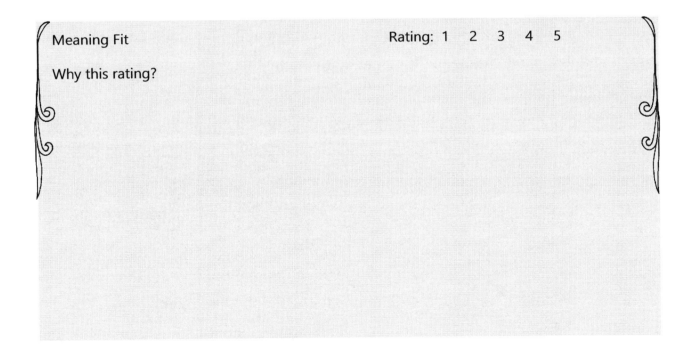

Meaning Fit   Rating: 1   2   3   4   5

Why this rating?

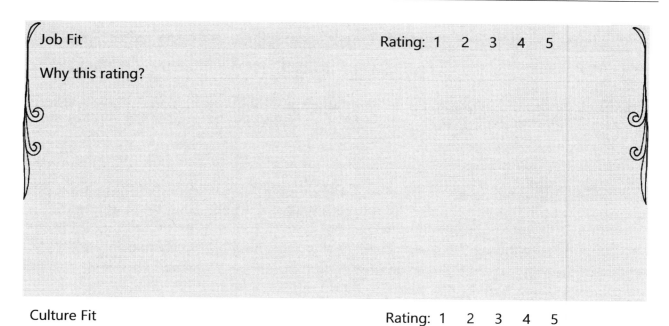

Job Fit

Rating: 1 2 3 4 5

Why this rating?

Culture Fit

Rating: 1 2 3 4 5

Why this rating?

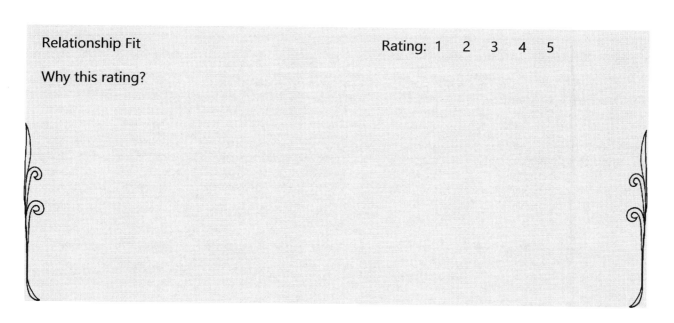

Relationship Fit

Rating: 1 2 3 4 5

Why this rating?

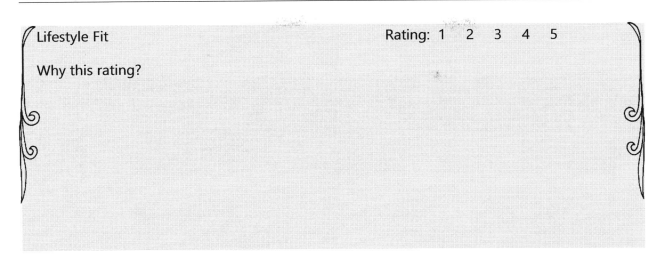

Lifestyle Fit   Rating: 1 2 3 4 5

Why this rating?

Financial Fit   Rating: 1 2 3 4 5

Why this rating?

What are you thinking and feeling right now? _____

_____

_____

_____

What else is contributing to your desire for a new job or career? _____

_____

_____

_____

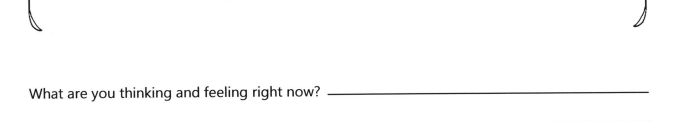

You're doing great. Now comes the fun part. It's time for some big-picture, blue-sky thinking! For an open, relaxed mindset, start by getting your markers or colored pencils and coloring the next page.

Big Picture, Blue Sky Thinking

What Does Big-Picture, Blue-Sky Thinking Have to Do with Your Career?

So often when we think about changing jobs or careers, we begin with our immediate goals in mind—especially when we're going through difficult times. In the process, we limit our thinking to a single step on the career ladder instead of (a) taking our long-term wishes and dreams into account, and (b) thinking two or three career moves out to get us where we want to go.

By considering our wishes and dreams in the actual career-planning process, we can
- radically expand our field of vision
- more strategically plan the next two or three steps in our career
- simultaneously work to accomplish our wishes and dreams

Additionally, we can build greater balance into our lives if we factor in the *memories we want to make* with our families and friends—as well as for ourselves.

So, what would it be like to incorporate your wishes, dreams, and desired memories into the career-planning process? How would that feel to you? _____

_____

_____

_____

_____

_____

_____

What would be the upsides and downsides of considering them as you develop your career plans?

_____

_____

_____

_____

_____

_____

How would actively incorporating "blue sky thinking" into your next job or career change alter your career-planning approach going forward?

_____

_____

_____

_____

_____

_____

_____

To what extent are you willing to give it a try? (1 = If I Absolutely Must; 10 = Let's Do This!)

1   2   3   4   5   6   7   8   9   10

What would it take to increase this score by one or two steps? _____

_____

_____

_____

_____

_____

_____

Your "Bucket List" of Wishes

Let's begin by making a list of all the fun and rewarding things you would like to do, experience, and accomplish in your lifetime. Want to try skydiving? Write it down. Want to volunteer at a wildlife sanctuary in Costa Rica? Capture it here. Go ahead—dream big. What would make your life extraordinary? Here's some space where you can brainstorm ideas. The secret to the power of this exercise is to let your imagination run wild.

Now, review the ideas that you generated and identify your *top three wishes* in the following space:

#1) _____

#2) _____

#3) _____

Get...ready...for...it.... What specific steps would you need to take to accomplish *each* of your top three wishes? (No kidding. We're doing this thing here and now!) Here's an example:

> My Wish: Skydive
>
> Step 1: Conduct research about skydiving on Google or Bing
>
> Step 2: Identify at least one reputable skydiving operation near where I live
>
> Step 3: Learn where and when skydiving lessons are offered; drive there and observe
>
> Step 4: Try a tandem dive to see if I enjoy the experience
>
> Step 5: If yes, save up and sign up for skydiving lessons

It's your turn. On the following pages, identify 5–7 steps you would need to take to accomplish your top three wishes. Don't be afraid to dive into this question. If you're feeling anything other than fearless, consider the exercise to be an interesting thought experiment.

Wish #1: _____

Step 1:

Step 2:

Step 3:

Step 4:

Step 5:

Step 6:

Step 7:

Wish #2: _____

Step 1:

Step 2:

Step 3:

Step 4:

Step 5:

Step 6:

Step 7:

Wish #3: ——————————————————————————————————————

Step 1:

Step 2:

Step 3:

Step 4:

Step 5:

Step 6:

Step 7:

Just out of curiosity, what are the *chances* that you could make of each of your three wishes come true in the next 3–5 years if you committed yourself to completing each of the steps?

Wish #1	Low	Moderate	High
Wish #2	Low	Moderate	High
Wish #3	Low	Moderate	High

What's stopping you?

_____

_____

_____

_____

_____

What's one step you could take this week to start making each of your wishes come true?

Wish #1: I could _____

_____

_____

_____

_____

Wish #2: I could _____

_____

_____

_____

_____

Wish #3: I could _____

_____

_____

_____

_____

Three Years from Now

There's a lot of talk about "following our dreams." Believe me, I'm all in. How about you?

The important thing to remember about accomplishing dreams—particularly BIG ones—is that doing so begins with creating a crystal-clear vision.

A powerful way to help you articulate your vision is to complete the following assignment, developed by world-class, high-performance coach Rich Litvin.

Fast-forward in your mind to three years from today's date. Imagine yourself reaching for your cell phone to call an old friend with whom you've lost touch. You're excited about catching up and sharing stories about interesting places you've visited, fun things you've done, and extraordinary accomplishments you've achieved in your career in the past three years. Without placing any limits on your imagination—and without any guilt for dreaming, what stories would you like to share during that conversation?

Use the following page to brainstorm your thoughts about *the amazing life you are living three years from now.*

Feel free to incorporate your top three wishes from the previous exercise. For added fun, try your hand at drawing or "mind mapping" your vision.*

---

* *Mind mapping is a simple, creative way to capture words, concepts, ideas, or tasks in a visual, graphic form. For more information, check out this website:* *https://www.mindmapping.com/*

Brainstorming Session

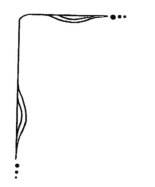

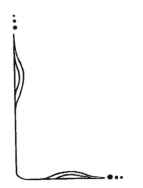

Now, let's take a closer look at your brainstorming notes and see if we can tease out the key elements of your vision.

By the end of Year #3,

1. Interesting places I've visited

  _____

  _____

  _____

  _____

  _____

2. Fun things I've done

  _____

  _____

  _____

  _____

  _____

3. Extraordinary accomplishments I've achieved

  _____

  _____

  _____

  _____

  _____

Hmmmm. Compelling stuff. Next, "zoom in" more closely on the vision you've created for yourself and convert your ideas into five goal statements. Here are two examples, which reflect the visions of artist Bonnie Sales and myself. (Bonnie is the wildly talented illustrator of this book).

Bonnie's dream three years from now:

1. Participate in art shows and exhibits
2. Sell my art patterns to textile makers for interior designers and decorators
3. Sell my own children's books and greeting cards
4. Have art in the homes of Tony Robbins, Dean Graziosi, and Lisa Ober
5. Visit Greece for the third time in three years

Deb's dream three years from now:

1. Spend three months of the year living in Ireland with my husband
    a. Walk the countryside, journaling and blogging about the experience
    b. Read Irish literature and poetry
2. Spend the remaining months living, working, playing, and marathon training at our home in Missouri
3. Coach 10–12 high-performing clients at any given time throughout the year
4. Run the Dublin Marathon

Your turn! Three years from now, YOUR dream is to

1.

2.

3.

4.

5.

Whoa, what just happened? What thoughts and emotions did you experience while you were completing this exercise?

Let's see what happens if you map out the steps to accomplish these goals using the exercise on the following page. If you need to take a quick break, then have a little fun with this maze.

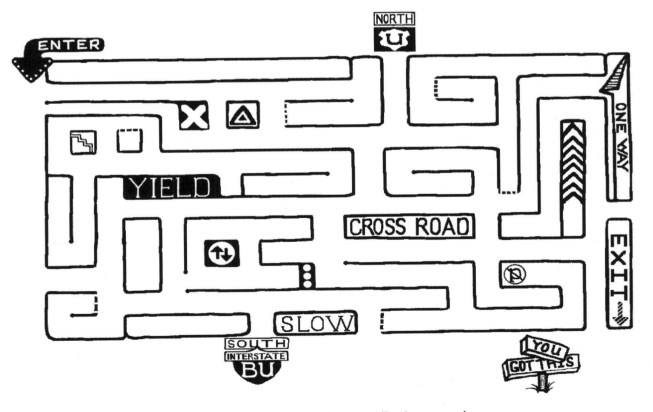

What Would It Take to Achieve Your Three-Year Vision?

Now's the time for the proverbial rubber to meet the road and figure out the *high-level steps* to achieve your three-year vision. Don't let yourself be daunted. Completing this exercise simply means working backward from Year #3 and identifying the steps you will need to have completed by (a) two years from now, (b) one year from now, (c) six months from now, (d) three months from now, and (e) one month from now.

Just breathe! This exercise is supposed to be fun. Sit back, relax, and enjoy the experience. To help you get started, Bonnie and I have worked through this exercise to provide you with two examples. You will find our answers on the following pages.

As you'll see, the process begins with the five goal statements that you generated in the previous exercise.

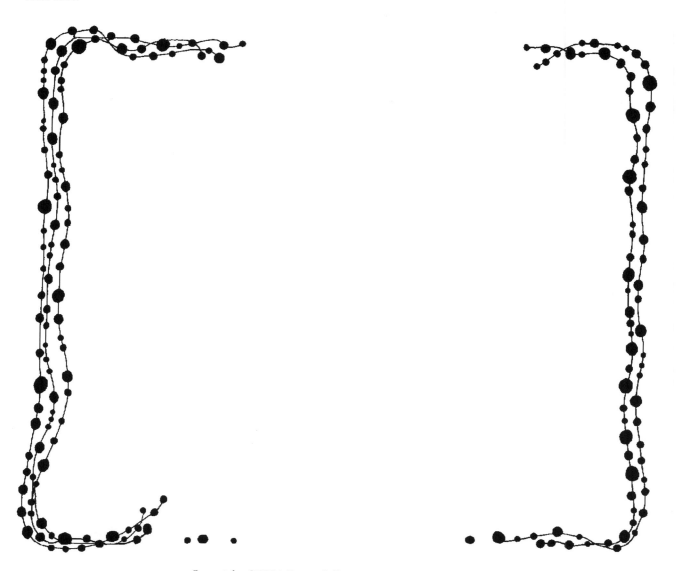

Example #1: Bonnie's Three-Year Vision

Three years from now, my dream is to

1. Participate in art shows and exhibits, with up to 36 original works of art (1 per month)
2. Sell my art patterns to textile makers for interior designers and decorators
3. Sell my own children's books and greeting cards
4. Have my art in the homes of Tony Robbins, Dean Graziosi, and Lisa Ober
5. Visit Greece for the third time in three years

To achieve my three-year vision,

Two years from now, I will have

1. Created 24 original works of art for shows or exhibits (1 per month)
2. Published a children's book series
3. Created and published a greeting card line
4. Prepared for my first art show or exhibit
5. Vacationed in Greece for the second time

One year from now, I will have

1. Created 12 original works of art for shows or exhibits (1 per month)
2. Contacted artists and gallery owners to see what I need to do to show my work
3. Learned pattern design and begun selling my textile designs on Spoonflower
4. Written storylines and completed illustrations for my children's book series
5. Vacationed in Greece for the first time

Six months from now, I will have

1. Created 6 original works of art for shows or exhibits (1 per month)
2. Launched a home-staging side business to generate additional income
3. Built a following for my artwork online at Merch by Amazon, Red Bubble, and Teespring
4. Made travel arrangements for my first trip to Greece

Three months from now, I will have

1. Created 3 original works of art for shows or exhibits (1 per month)
2. Shadowed a successful home stager to learn the ropes
3. Begun to sell my artwork online at Merch by Amazon, Red Bubble, Teespring
4. Learned to advertise my online sales
5. Researched places I would love to visit and stay in Greece

One month from now, I will have

1. Completed 1 original work of art for a show or exhibit
2. Talked with builders, stagers, and realtors about creating a home-staging side business
3. Created artwork and uploaded my designs at Merch by Amazon, Red Bubble, and Teespring
4. Set up a savings account for annual trips to Greece and started making monthly deposits

Example #2: Deb's Three-Year Vision

Three years from now, my dream is to

1. Spend 3 months out of the year living in Ireland with my husband
   a. Walk the countryside, journaling and blogging about the experience
   b. Read Irish literature and poetry
2. Spend the remaining months living, working, playing, and marathon training at our home in Missouri
3. Coach 10 high-performing clients at any given time throughout the year
4. Run the Dublin Marathon

To achieve my three-year vision,

Two years from now, I will have

1. Tried on my Irish dream for size for 3–4 weeks and scouted locations to live next year
2. Coached a minimum of 7 high-performing clients at a time throughout the year
3. Developed a social media following on my blog as well as on LinkedIn and Twitter
4. Run a full marathon

One year from now, I will have

1. Vacationed with my husband for 10–12 days in two or three different parts of Ireland
2. Created 10–12 new coaching clients
3. Had fun creating a powerful coaching blog and regularly posting on LinkedIn and Twitter
4. Run a half marathon

Six months from now, I will have

1. Planned a 10–12-day Irish vacation with my husband for next year
2. Created 5–6 new coaching clients
3. Regularly posted on LinkedIn and Twitter
4. Commenced training for a half-marathon

Three months from now, I will have

1. Researched places to visit for a 10–12-day Irish vacation
2. Published and successfully launched *Morph, Pivot, Launch*
3. Run 10K (6.2 miles) as my long run once a week
4. Created 2–3 new coaching clients
5. Studied *Living and Working in Ireland* by J. Laredo

One month from now, I will have

1. Finished the final draft of *Morph, Pivot, Launch*
2. Completed my first 6-mile run
3. Finished reading the book *Circle of Friends* by beloved Irish novelist Maeve Binchy
4. Started a savings account for my Irish dream and begun to make monthly deposits

YOUR Three-Year Vision

Three years from now, my dream is: (Copy your five goal statements from the previous exercise)

1.

2.

3.

4.

5.

To achieve my three-year vision,

Two years from now, I will have

1.

2.

3.

4.

5.

One year from now, I will have

1.

2.

3.

4.

5.

Six months from now, I will have

1.

2.

3.

4.

5.

Three months from now, I will have

1.

2.

3.

4.

5.

One month from now, I will have

1.

2.

3.

4.

5.

Wow! What does that feel like? _____

_____

_____

_____

If you committed yourself completely to accomplishing this plan, what are the chances you could make it come true in the next three years?

_____

_____

_____

How would you feel if you put this game plan into motion as part of your career plans?

_____

_____

_____

_____

_____

_____

What would your career objectives look like if this game plan was part of the calculus? Would your objectives change or stay the same? In what ways?

_____

_____

_____

_____

_____

_____

_____

_____

_____

_____

What steps could you take to help sustain your energy, engagement, and actions while you are working toward accomplishing your vision?

_____
_____
_____
_____
_____
_____
_____
_____

What could stop you from moving forward with this plan? How could you overcome these potential challenges?

_____
_____
_____
_____
_____
_____
_____
_____

Memories You Want to Make

Articulating your wishes and dreams is a useful way to conceptualize your desired future. So, too, is "flipping the script" and focusing on the memories you would like to make. Doing so can help you to maintain a sense of equilibrium and focus on the life you want to lead—a more "in the moment" approach to planning your future.

So, here's the question: What memories do you want to make with your *family* in the next six months? Next year? Next three years?

_____

_____

_____

_____

_____

_____

_____

_____

What memories do you want to make with your *friends?*

_____

_____

_____

_____

_____

_____

_____

_____

What memories do you want to make for *yourself* in these five areas of life?

    a. Working:

    b. Playing:

    c. Creating:

    d. Learning:

    e. Giving back to the world:

How would your life be different if you began to regularly schedule time in your calendar to make these specific memories?

_____

_____

_____

_____

_____

_____

_____

How would you tweak your vision (i.e., five goal statements) to include your desired memories? (Feel free to use the space below for your revision.)

My Revised Vision Statement:

Three years from now, my dream is to

1.

2.

3.

4.

5.

Your Dream Job

This activity is designed to help you explore your dream job, including your passions, purpose, ideal day, and "destination bliss." Take your time answering these questions. You'll learn much about yourself that can inform your next career move. If you need a break part-way through the exercise, stop and stretch. Then return and bring your best energy to the exercise.

If you could have any job in the world, what would it be—given your wishes, dreams, and vision for the future?

_____
_____
_____
_____
_____

Why would you love to have this job?

_____
_____
_____
_____
_____

What would be the upsides and downsides of this job?

Upsides   **Downsides**

_____   _____
_____   _____
_____   _____
_____   _____
_____   _____
_____   _____
_____   _____

What are your favorite hobbies or pastimes, and why do you love them?

_____

_____

_____

_____

_____

_____

To what extent are your hobbies or pastimes related to your dream job? (Please explain if related.)

_____

_____

_____

_____

_____

_____

_____

What do you believe is your purpose or reason for being in this world—your why?

_____

_____

_____

_____

_____

_____

To what extent is your purpose related to your dream job?

_____

_____

_____

_____

_____

_____

If you could work anywhere in the world (any city, state, region, country, or part of the world), where would you work and why? Let's call this your "destination bliss."

_____

_____

_____

_____

_____

What is your perfect average workday? Break down what you would be doing hour by hour from the moment you awaken until the time you go to sleep. (Yes! Absolutely, you can sleep until 10 a.m.)

5 a.m.   _____

6 a.m.   _____

7 a.m.   _____

8 a.m.   _____

9 a.m.   _____

10 a.m.   _____

11 a.m.   _____

12 a.m.   _____

1 p.m.   _____

2 p.m.   _____

3 p.m.   _____

4 p.m.   _____

5 p.m.   _____

6 p.m.   _____

7 p.m.   _____

8 p.m.   _____

9 p.m.   _____

Take a moment and reflect on your answers to the questions in this exercise. What happens to your overall energy and enthusiasm when you think about the possibilities?

_____

_____

_____

_____

_____

Beginning now, what specific step(s) could you take both personally and professionally that could move you closer to

- Landing or creating your dream job:

- Incorporating your favorite hobbies and pastimes into your career or professional life:

- Fulfilling your life's purpose:

- Crafting your perfect average day:

- Achieving your Destination Bliss:

What's stopping you from taking these specific step(s) toward

- Landing or creating your dream job: _____
_____
_____
_____
_____
_____
_____

- Incorporating your favorite hobbies and pastimes into your career or professional life:

  _____

  _____

  _____

  _____

  _____

  _____

- Fulfilling your life's purpose: _____

  _____

  _____

  _____

  _____

  _____

  _____

- Crafting your perfect average day: _____

  _____

  _____

  _____

  _____

  _____

  _____

- Achieving your Destination Bliss: _____

  _____

  _____

  _____

  _____

  _____

  _____

What could you do to overcome these challenges?

1.

2.

3.

4.

5.

6.

7.

Having completed this exercise, what did you learn about yourself that could guide you in taking your next big career step? _____

_____

_____

_____

_____

_____

_____

_____

_____

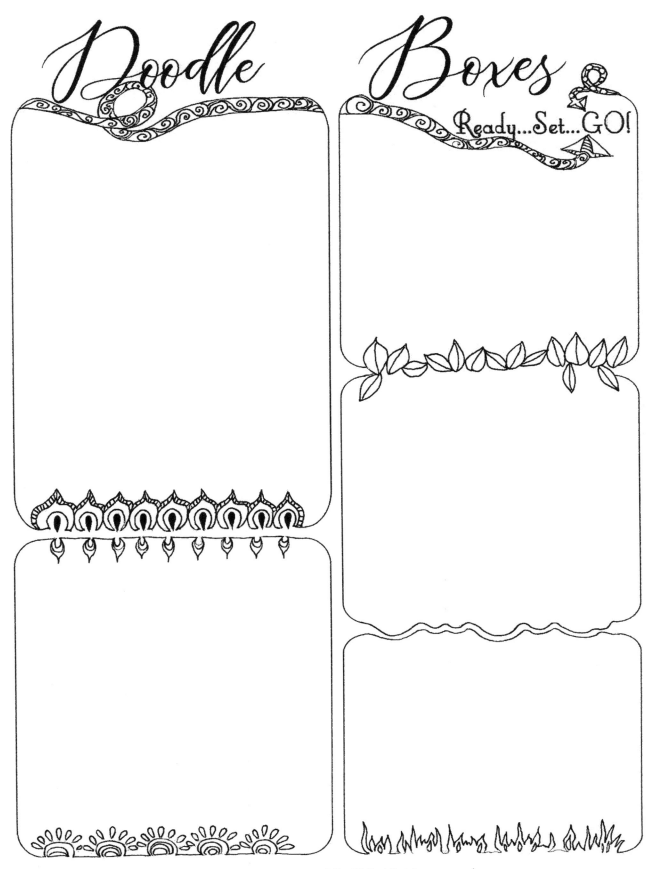

Morph, Pivot, Launch

So often when we're ready for a new job or career, we experience "tunnel vision" regarding the options that are available. For example, we may limit the scope of our search to positions, titles, or work roles that are identical to our current (or most recent) position, rather than broadening the aperture to include a wider variety of opportunities.

In fact, there are numerous possibilities. You could....

- Change *positions, titles, or work roles* in your current company or organization. For example, you could apply for promotion to a supervisory or management position or pursue a lateral career move (e.g., from Human Resources to Marketing). You also could transition from full-time to part-time or contract work, or vice versa.

- Change *cities, regions, or countries* while staying with your current employer. Doing so would allow you to make major personal or professional changes without leaving the work and company you enjoy. Here your goal might be Destination Bliss. Three options you could explore are a short-term assignment in another office location; a month away, during which you work remotely from anywhere in the world; or a permanent transfer.

- Change *companies or organizations* but stick with your current work role. For instance, you could continue growing your career as an account manager in the field of advertising, but "pivot" from a traditional advertising firm to a new and exciting ad agency in the start-up phase.

- Change *industries* while remaining with your current work role. To illustrate, you might continue your career as a professional tax accountant but transition from the business services industry to a not-for-profit organization about which you're passionate.

- Change *everything,* including your work role, company, industry, and (possibly) location. This decision is potentially the biggest, hairiest, scariest change possible. For example, you might leave a mid-level or senior-management position with the Federal government to work full-time for an international non-governmental organization, or NGO. Or you might go back to school and pursue a new certification, degree, or apprenticeship.

- Develop a "side hustle" (entrepreneurial venture) or do freelance projects on the side—often pursued by people who want to build an off-ramp from one career to another. For example, you could sell your own products or services online; do freelance work, such as technical writing, graphic design, proposal development, bookkeeping, etc.; or teach evenings or weekends at a local community college or university.

To ensure that you're maximizing the number of opportunities available to you, let's take a closer look at each of these possibilities and how you feel about them via the next exercise.

Notes

I. Morph

Possibility #1: Change positions, titles, or work roles in your current company

On a scale of 1–10, how ready are you to take on different roles or responsibilities in your current company? (1=Low; 10=High)

1   2   3   4   5   6   7   8   9   10

What interesting or satisfying opportunities could you pursue without leaving the company? Think outside the box. Consider potential talent-development programs, sabbaticals you could pursue, new projects you could lead, promotions you could go after, lateral moves you might make, and part-time or contract work you could do.

Brainstorm possible options in the space below.

Based on your brainstorming session, rank in order your top three professional development or job opportunities with your current company or organization:

1. _____

2. _____

3. _____

What specific steps would you need to take in order pursue each of these opportunities?

Steps to Pursue Opportunity #1:

-
-
-
-
-

Steps to Pursue Opportunity #2:

-
-
-
-
-

Steps to Pursue Opportunity #3:

-
-
-
-
-

Name three people whom you could ask to serve as advocates or mentors as you pursue one or more of these opportunities. Why these three people? How could they help you the most?

Mentor/Advocate #1: _____

Why? How could he or she help? _____

_____

_____

_____

_____

_____

_____

Mentor/Advocate #2: _____

Why? How could he or she help? _____

_____

_____

_____

_____

_____

_____

Mentor/Advocate #3: _____

Why? How could he or she help? _____

_____

_____

_____

_____

_____

_____

Having completed this exercise, what are you thinking and feeling right now?

What next step would you like to take to move forward, if any?

What obstacles could get in your way?

What plan could you put into place to overcome these obstacles?

Possibility #2: Change cities, regions, or countries while staying with your current employer

This possibility is based on three assumptions: (1) you love what you do and enjoy working for your present company and either (2) your company has offices in more than one location *and* you have opportunities to relocate, or (3) your company has a very forward-thinking remote working policy and you can work your current job from anywhere in the world.

Assuming you can check two out of these three boxes, to what extent do you believe a "change in scenery" would help you to achieve greater personal and professional growth? To address these questions,

A. Rate your potential for *personal* growth as a function of such a move, based on the following 7-point scale (1 = Very Little Growth, 7 = Exceptional Growth):

1   2   3   4   5   6   7

In what specific ways do you think this change would significantly increase your *personal* growth and development?

1.

2.

3.

B. Now, rate your potential for *professional* growth, based on the same 7-point scale (1=Very Little Growth, 7 = Exceptional Growth)

1   2   3   4   5   6   7

How do you think such a change would significantly increase your *professional* growth and development?

1.

2.

3.

In what other cities, states, provinces, regions, or countries does your company have offices (or where you would want to live and work from remotely)? If three or more locations, list and rank in order your top three here. Circle your number one choice.

#1: ————————————————————————————————————

#2: ————————————————————————————————————

#3: ————————————————————————————————————

What steps could you take now with management or senior leaders to start the conversation about a possible transfer, short-term assignment, or remote working?

a.

b.

c.

Whom in management or leadership could you recruit as ambassadors to help you make this dream a reality?

Person #1 _____

Person #2 _____

Person #3 _____

What obstacles could stand in your way of pursuing such a change?

- _____
  _____
  _____
  _____
  _____
  _____

- _____
  _____
  _____
  _____
  _____
  _____

- _____
  _____
  _____
  _____
  _____
  _____

What steps could you take to overcome these obstacles?

To overcome Obstacle #1:

To overcome Obstacle #2:

To overcome Obstacle #3:

On a scale of 1–10, how committed are you to giving it a try? (1 = Uh, no! 10=Hell, yeah!)
Your rating: —————

II. Pivot

Possibility #3: Change companies or organizations but stick with your current work role

If you could work for any three (3) companies or organizations in the world, what would they be and why would you like to work for them?

1. Company/Organization: _____ Why? _____

   _____

   _____

   _____

   _____

2. Company/Organization: _____ Why? _____

   _____

   _____

   _____

   _____

3. Company/Organization: _____ Why? _____

   _____

   _____

   _____

   _____

What unique knowledge, skills, and abilities could you offer each of these companies?

Company/Organization #1: _____

_____

_____

_____

_____

_____

Company/Organization #2: _____

_____

_____

_____

_____

_____

Company/Organization #3: _____

_____

_____

_____

_____

_____

What *new* knowledge, skills, and abilities would you need to cultivate for a similar position, title, or work role to significantly increase your chances of landing a job with each company? (Take your time with this question. Talk with friends and colleagues in your field. You may be surprised by what you learn.)

Company/Organization #1: _____

_____

_____

_____

_____

_____

Company/Organization #2: _____

_____

_____

_____

_____

_____

Company/Organization #3: —————————————————————————

_____

_____

_____

_____

_____

What research plan could you put into place to gather information about each of these companies or organizations as well as similar positions that currently are available?

What would an offer look like from one of these three companies or organizations that you would characterize as "a better offer" than your current position?

_____

_____

_____

_____

_____

_____

_____

_____

_____

_____

What's stopping you from checking out each of these companies or organizations now?

_____

_____

_____

_____

_____

_____

_____

_____

How could you overcome these obstacles?

_____

_____

_____

_____

_____

_____

_____

_____

_____

Possibility #4: Change industries while remaining with your current work role

The number of different industries (and market segments within each industry) that you can explore is truly mind-boggling. Following is a list of the 18 major U.S. industries, with the number of individual market segments comprising each industry tallied in parentheses. Place a check mark in the box beside any industry that you would like to explore.

☐ Accommodation & Food Services (13)
☐ Administration, Business Support, or Waste Management (26)
☐ Agriculture, Forestry, Fishing, and Hunting (30)
☐ Arts, Entertainment, and Recreation (20)
☐ Construction (37)
☐ Educational Services (14)
☐ Finance and Insurance (32)
☐ Health Care and Social Assistance (34)
☐ Information (39)
☐ Manufacturing (194)
☐ Mining (11)
☐ Other Services Except Public Administration (29)
☐ Professional, Scientific, and Technical Services (36)
☐ Real Estate and Rental/Leasing (20)
☐ Retail Trade (64)
☐ Transportation/Warehousing (38)
☐ Utilities (11)
☐ Wholesale Trade (68)

Please note that myriad possibilities exist if you take a deep dive into the many market segments associated with each industry. For example, the Accommodation and Food Services Industry alone is comprised of 13 market segments: bars and nightclubs; bed & breakfast and hostel accommodations; campgrounds and RV parks; casino hotels; caterers; chain restaurants; coffee and snack shops; fast food restaurants; food service contractors; hotels and motels; single, full-service restaurants; vendors; and tourism.

Before deciding to completely change industries, you may want to explore individual market segments within your current industry.

For more information about these 18 industries and their respective market segments, check out IbisWorld.com at **https://www.ibisworld.com/united-states/list-of-industries/**

IbisWorld is considered one of the most thoroughly researched, reliable, and authoritative sources of market information in the world.

III. Launch

Possibility #5: Change everything, including your work, company, industry, and (possibly) location

In the career world, we have a highly technical term for this possibility: *Jump!*

If you've ever daydreamed about making such a bold move, then we strongly recommend checking out Mike Lewis's practical, engaging, and informative guidebook, *When to Jump: If the Job You Have Isn't the Life You Want.*

What we love most about Lewis's book is its four-phase guiding framework, which he calls "The Jump Curve," and 44 inspiring case studies of people like you and me who have successfully made a jump. In short, this book is a must-read if you're considering jumping as a possibility.

To determine if your next step is to IMMEDIATELY go out and purchase Lewis's book, let's use this journal space to tease a few of his most important points.

What do you dream about doing every day of your life—from the time you get up in the morning until the time you go to sleep at night—if only you weren't afraid?

What financial plan could you put into place that would make it possible to pursue your dream in the next 3–5 years? (Jot down a couple of preliminary notes here.)

Extra Notes

In what ways could you use your vacation time, "comp time," lunch times, break times, and every waking moment of your spare time to try out your dream without giving up your current, full-time job?

What safety net could you put into place in case your jump fails?

On a scale of 1–10 (1 = Never; 10 = Always), how often do you see opportunities in failures that you encounter in life?

1   2   3   4   5   6   7   8   9   10

Provide at least one example of a time when you have turned a spectacular failure into an opportunity:

_____

_____

_____

_____

_____

_____

How did you turn things around?

_____

_____

_____

_____

_____

_____

Overall, how inclined are you to spend more time looking toward the future rather than the past

    1 = Significantly more inclined to look toward the future

    2 = Somewhat more inclined to look toward the future

    3 = About 50/50 toward the future and past

    4 = Somewhat more inclined to focus on the past

    5 = Significantly more inclined to focus on the past

My rating: _____

If your rating was a 3, 4, 5, how willing and able are you to start focusing more on your future rather than dwelling on the past?

_____

_____

_____

_____

_____

What strategies could you put into place to try out your dream and practice living in the Now?

If you found these questions to be interesting and compelling—especially if you're considering a jump, then head to your favorite book retailer and purchase *When to Jump!* Then promise yourself to read the book from cover to cover before making your next career move.

We also recommend checking out Lewis's excellent website for some great resources. Here's a link: **http://www.whentojump.com/**

Possibility #6: Develop a "side hustle" (entrepreneurial venture) or do freelance projects while keeping your regular job

Have you ever dreamed of starting your own business "on the side" or doing freelance work to supplement your income?

According to side-hustle guru Chris Guillebeau, there are three broad categories of side hustles:

- Selling products
    - Tangible products (handcrafted furniture, gourmet ice cream, self-care products)
    - Intangible products (newsletters, webinars, memberships in online communities)
- Providing services (pet sitting, personal chef, mystery shopping, Zoom support)
- Improving existing products or services (reselling products online, making a better widget)[37]

Many side hustles start with a favorite hobby, passion, or talent (e.g., painting, woodworking, writing, photography). Others emerge when we see an opportunity in the market that nobody is filling (e.g., stand-in-line service, online music lessons, or sports coaching for kids via Zoom).

What do YOU love to do for fun? What are you passionate about—i.e., what excites you, fills you up, and feeds your soul? What are your special talents?

Feel free to use the space below to capture your thoughts:

Based on your brainstorming session, list and rank in order your top three hobbies, passions, or talents that you could turn into additional income. Be creative! You never know what's possible until you dream.

Hobby, Passion, or Talent #1: _____

How could you turn this into extra income?

Hobby, Passion, or Talent #2: _____

How could you turn this into extra income?

Hobby, Passion, or Talent #3: _____

How could you turn this into extra income?

How would you feel about starting your own side hustle or doing freelance projects for additional income?

What would be the pros and cons?

Pros	Cons
_____	_____
_____	_____
_____	_____
_____	_____
_____	_____
_____	_____
_____	_____
_____	_____
_____	_____
_____	_____
_____	_____

Who in your network has launched a side hustle or does freelance work who could share credible advice and guidance about the subject?

On a scale of 1–10, how interested are you in talking with at least two (2) such people in your network? (1=Are you crazy? No way; 10 = Yep, I'm that crazy—WAY!)

1   2   3   4   5   6   7   8   9   10

What would it take to make the phone calls?

Heads up! An excellent source of information about launching a business on the side is Chris Guillebeau's *Side Hustle: From Idea to Income in 27 Days*.

For those with an entrepreneurial bent but unsure about where to begin, another great resource is Guillebeau's *100 Side Hustles: Unexpected Ways for Making Money Without Quitting Your Day Job*. Both books are chock full of practical advice and ideas.

If you're not interested in starting a new company, but like the idea of doing freelance projects, a good place to begin is by listing your services online. A few well-known sites include FlexJobs, SolidGigs, Fiverr, Upwork, and Indeed. For a more complete listing, check out Ryan Robinson's excellent article, "78 Best Freelance Job Websites to Get Remote Freelance Work (Fast) in 2020," at **https://www.ryrob.com/freelance-jobs/**

Building an Effective Off-Ramp

What does "building an effective off-ramp" look like as relates to a job or career change? Doing so involves planning and preparing for your exit by ensuring that you have the financial means to sustain yourself throughout the process, and gracefully exiting your company while burning as few bridges as possible (i.e., preserving meaningful and important relationships).

Even if you've already left your current job or career, the next tool may help you to plan your way forward.

Your Financial Off-Ramp

For some people, building an effective financial off-ramp requires keeping your current job while conducting a job search. Doing so affords you the opportunity to look for a position without jeopardizing your current income. Clearly, this approach is the ideal solution, and you will want to stay in place for as long as possible.

For others, personal or professional circumstances may not afford this luxury. For example, you are (a) fired or laid off from a job; (b) moving to another city, state, or country with a spouse or partner who has landed a dream job; (c) facing health- or family-related issues requiring you to change your work situation; or (d) dealing with an extraordinarily toxic workplace that is exacting an extreme toll on your health. (Note: Many viable ways exist for you to generate income, even in these perilous situations. More on this subject in a moment.)

In whatever circumstances you find yourself, you need to build an effective financial management plan to sustain you throughout your job or career change—one that's driven by the amount of money it takes to pay your monthly bills and live as frugally as possible. You also need to know where your money will come from as you progress through your search.

On the following two pages is a worksheet to help you create a monthly budget. (Don't panic! You can do this.) If you prefer to go the technology route, you can also drop these expenses into a simple Excel spreadsheet or use an app like Intuit Mint to create a monthly budget. For more information about Mint, here's a link: **https://www.mint.com/how-mint-works/budgets**

Take the time and energy NOW to complete this exercise. Doing so will help you to assess the reality of your situation and make better decisions about ways to generate income as you search for your next job or launch a new career.

Expense Type	Average Monthly Costs
House payment or rent	
Homeowners association fees	
Electricity	
Water	
Garbage	
Sewage	
Cable/internet	
Telephone	
Car payment	
Gasoline	
Groceries	
Insurance	
Auto	
Home	
Life	
Health	
Vision	
Dental	
Monthly credit card bills	
Medical bills	
Prescription drugs	
Pets	
Veterinary care	

Notes

Expense Type	Average Monthly Costs
Taxes	
Misc. (Add other expenses here)	
Clothing allowance	
Eating out	
Digital entertainment (e.g., Netflix)	
(Other)	
(Other)	
(Other)	
TOTAL MONTHLY BUDGET	

Notes

If you don't currently employ a monthly budget like this one, you may be experiencing "sticker shock." However, knowing how much you spend each month helps you know the amount of income you need to sustain yourself through both your job search and first month on the job.

For example, if your current monthly expenses total to $3,000, then you will need to make sure that you can generate $18,000 of income if your job search takes six months ($3,000 per month x 6 months = $18,000). Add an additional $3,000 of living expenses to pay your bills from the time you accept a new position until you receive your first paycheck, usually two-to-four weeks on the job. Using this formula, the grand total you will need to generate is $21,000 ($18,000 + $3,000 = $21,000).

Based on your assessment, how much money do you need each month to pay your bills and live frugally?

$ _____ per month

Assuming your job search takes six months, how much income will you need to cover your living expenses for that 6-month period plus your first month on the job?

$ _____ for a total of 7 months

Having completed this exercise, what are you thinking?

_____

_____

_____

_____

_____

_____

How are you feeling about your job or career change from a money perspective (e.g., surprised, excited, concerned, frustrated, dismayed)?

_____

_____

_____

_____

_____

_____

Let's keep going! In the next exercise, we'll work through a number of possible income sources and categorize them by risk level.

Ways to Make Money

Generating income can seem exceptionally daunting, especially if you're going through difficult times.

However, with a little imagination, you can make money in a variety of ways—keeping in mind that some ways are riskier than others. Here's a diagram that categorizes possible income sources according to risk:

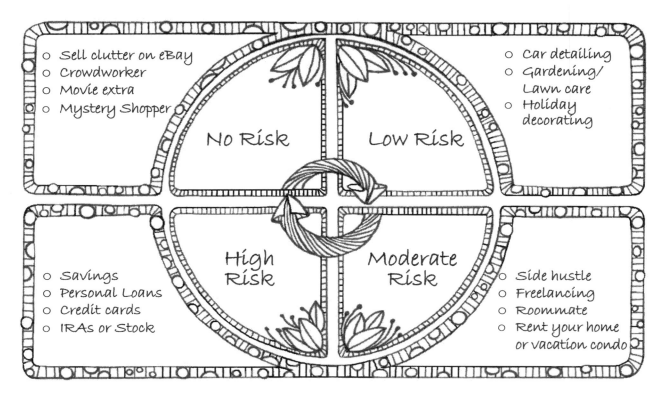

No Risk

In his 2020 article entitled "40 Easy Ways to Make Money Quickly," Owen Burek offered readers several intriguing, risk-free ways to make money. A few of our favorites include

- Clearing and selling your clutter on Craigslist, Ebay, or other online sites, including books, movies, games, CDs, and old phones—as well as gold or silver jewelry you no longer wear
- Selling your photos to Getty Images or Adobe Stock
- Getting paid to take online surveys, search the web, review websites and apps, and write product descriptions as a "crowdworker" via the web platform Amazon Mechanical Turk
- Becoming a movie extra or mystery shopper[38]

For more information, check out Burek's article at **https://www.savethestudent.org/make-money/10-quick-cash-injections.html**

What additional opportunities can you think of that would allow you to generate income with virtually no risk?

_____

_____

_____

_____

_____

_____

Low Risk

Several interesting, low-risk ways exist to generate income, including

- Securing a part-time job such as teaching online or at a local community college, becoming a bookseller at your favorite indie bookstore, or working in a gardening department or shop if you have a green thumb
- Offering home, car, or gardening services in your neighborhood, such as washing and detailing cars, decorating homes or boats for the holidays, organizing closets, or lawn and gardening work

The reason we classify these possibilities as "low risk" is that they include little or no up-front cash outlays. (If you have a full-time job and want to take on additional part-time work, you may want to ensure that your full-time employer will register no objections.)

What other creative ideas do you have for developing income that would require low risk?

_____

_____

_____

_____

_____

_____

_____

_____

Moderate Risk

In a previous exercise, we discussed "side hustles" and freelance work as two additional ways to generate supplemental income. The reason we are classifying them as moderately risky here is that they generally involve

- cash outlays to develop, launch, and market your products or services
- potential approval from your full-time employer

Other ways you could make money that are moderately risky are

- Taking on a roommate or renting out a room in your home (background check and three references mandatory)
- Renting your home, RV, or vacation condo on Airbnb (another Burek recommendation)

What other creative ideas do you have for generating income that would require moderate risk?

_____

_____

_____

_____

_____

_____

_____

High Risk

Because they directly impact your long-term financial security, the riskiest sources of income include

- Tapping into your savings
- Asking for personal loans from family or friends (Note: Consider potential effects on long-term relationships if not handled as a formal business arrangement.)
- Leveraging your home or car through an equity line of credit (or pawn shop)
- Using credit cards to pay your bills or taking out a personal or commercial bank loan
- Tapping into retirement accounts, IRAs, and stock portfolios

Before considering such high-risk moneymaking ventures, you should always consult with a trusted financial advisor.

What other creative sources of income can you think of without turning to a life of crime?

_____

_____

_____

_____

_____

_____

Only you know your level of risk tolerance. If you're comfortable with the amount of risk you are willing (or required) to take in order to change jobs or careers, then you can use your time, energy, and financial resources strategically to build an effective financial off-ramp.

If you are *uncomfortable* with the amount of risk that may be required, seek assistance from a reputable financial planner or financial management expert. He or she may be able to help.

Ready...Set...Go!

*W*hen you can't change the direction of the wind — adjust your sails.

H. Jackson Brown, Jr.

Acknowledgments

So many amazing people made this book possible. To each of you, we offer our sincerest, heartfelt gratitude and appreciation.

To the terrific writer and resume guru Kristen Edens, who contributed her smart, insightful "Job Hunting Tips to Beat Applicant Tracking Software (ATS)."

To the remarkable executive coach Christi Nix-Bloomer, who graciously shared her compelling CARMA model for "Making Decisions Throughout Your Job Search."

To our dearest friends and colleagues who read early drafts of the book and offered their thoughtful feedback and suggestions, including Eileen Perrigo, Christi Nix-Bloomer, Linda Smith, Kristen Edens, Sanam Parvizi, Renee Sinning, and Brian Lunt. And to the thoughtful, gracious Keith Vollmer (CPA) who offered valuable input on content related to financial planning.

To the inimitable Pat Dorsey of Mightier Than The Sword Consulting, our knowledgeable, patient book consultant extraordinaire, who first offered helpful advice and guidance during his excellent Author's Roundtable, then later shepherded the book through the many crazy steps associated with preparing and publishing the book. We couldn't have done this book without you.

To the brilliant Caren Libby, founder of Image Media, to whom we owe a debt of gratitude for her beautiful photography, exceptional website design and layout, and savvy digital-marketing strategy.

To the wildly creative marketing and social media maven, Mich Hancock with 100th Monkey Media, who led a fun, fabulous brainstorming session with us at the outset, which gave birth to the delightful tumblewing as our muse.

To our tireless, intrepid Army of Influencers on social media, who quickly spread the word that we were giving away the first two sections of the book, just as job losses were mounting around the world during the Global Pandemic, including Balinda Cakste, Keith Crabtree, Larry DeMoss, Rhonda Dobson, Pat Dorsey, Bob Dyrda, Kristen Edens, Kent Holland, Karen Hoffman, Alicen Holloway, Keith Krut, Caren Libby, Brian Lunt, Christi Nix-Bloomer, Peggy Neufeld, Sanam Parvizi, Eileen Perrigo, Chance Post, Renee Sinning, Linda Smith, Melissa Webber, and Kaitlin Wilson.

To trusted friend and therapist Jenna Barbosa, who served as a much-appreciated cheerleader and sounding board and who offered creative support throughout the design process.

To Deb's incredible husband, soul mate, and life partner David Gaut, who kept the earth spinning on its axis throughout the zany, maddening writing process.

Notes

Please note: We know that the internet is a place of constant change, and file locations and links are often revised. To keep things up to date for you, all current hyperlinks to our cited online resources are maintained on the *Morph, Pivot, Launch* website, MorphPivotLaunch.com.

1   Institute for Professional Excellence in Coaching. (2016, 2017a). *COR.E transitions dynamics: Foundations client workbook*, pp. 37, 46, 48, 50, 52, 53, 55, 56.

2   Institute for Professional Excellence in Coaching. (2016, 2017b). *COR.E transitions dynamics: Influencers client workbook*, pp. 8-9.

3   Institute for Professional Excellence in Coaching. (2016, 2017b). *COR.E transitions dynamics: Influencers client workbook*, p. 9.

4   Institute for Professional Excellence in Coaching. (2017) *The One Thing* [White paper], p. 1. http://morphpivotlaunch.com/.

5   Institute for Professional Excellence in Coaching. (2017). "5 Choices," p. 1. http://morphpivotlaunch.com/.

6   Institute for Professional Excellence in Coaching. (2016, 2017b). *COR.E transitions dynamics: Influencers client workbook*, p. 82.

7   Desired Effects Coaching (2020, July 20). "Catabolic vs. anabolic leaders – Part 4 – Big problem or huge opportunity," paras 1-4. http://morphpivotlaunch.com/.

8   Institute for Professional Excellence in Coaching. (2016, 2017b). *COR.E transitions dynamics: Influencers client workbook*, pp. 11-15.

9   Institute for Professional Excellence in Coaching. (2016, 2017a). *COR.E transitions dynamics: Foundations client workbook*, p. 71.

10   Institute for Professional Excellence in Coaching. (2016, 2017a). *COR.E transitions dynamics: Foundations client workbook*, p. 77.

11   Institute for Professional Excellence in Coaching. (2016, 2017a). *COR.E transitions dynamics: Foundations client workbook*, p. 78.

12   Institute for Professional Excellence in Coaching. (2016, 2017a). *COR.E transitions dynamics: Foundations client workbook*, p. 78.

13   Institute for Professional Excellence in Coaching. (2016, 2017a). *COR.E transitions dynamics: Foundations client workbook*, p. 75.

14   Institute for Professional Excellence in Coaching. (2016, 2017a). *COR.E transitions dynamics: Foundations client workbook*, p. 76.

15   Institute for Professional Excellence in Coaching. (2016, 2017a). *COR.E transitions dynamics: Foundations client workbook*, pp. 75-76.

16   Institute for Professional Excellence in Coaching. (2016, 2017a). *COR.E transitions dynamics: Foundations client workbook*, p. 73.

17   Institute for Professional Excellence in Coaching. (2016, 2017a). *COR.E transitions dynamics: Foundations client workbook*, p. 74.

18 Institute for Professional Excellence in Coaching. (2016, 2017a). *COR.E transitions dynamics: Foundations client workbook*, p. 71.

19 Institute for Professional Excellence in Coaching. (2016, 2017a). *COR.E transitions dynamics: Foundations client workbook*, p. 72.

20 Brown, B. (n.d.). Brené "Brown on how to reckon with emotion and change your narrative." *Oprah Magazine*. http://morphpivotlaunch.com/.

21 Jobscan. (n.d.) *Resume writing guide*. http://morphpivotlaunch.com/.

22 Etorama, C. (n.d.). "Customize your resume to stand out from the crowd." http://morphpivotlaunch.com/.

23 Purtill, C. (2020, April 9). "Feeling scatterbrained? Here's why." *The New York Times*, paras 1, 8. http://morphpivotlaunch.com/.

24 Torres, M. (2020, January 8). "How to make sure your new boss isn't terrible." *HuffPost*. http://morphpivotlaunch.com/.

25 Torres, M. (2020, January 8). "How to make sure your new boss isn't terrible." *HuffPost*, para 4. http://morphpivotlaunch.com/.

26 Finkle, J. (2019). *The introvert's complete guide: From landing a job to surviving, thriving, and moving on up*. Career Press, pp. 81-83.

27 Adeshola, A. (2020, March 19). "5 ways to stand out in your job search during the pandemic." *Forbes*. http://morphpivotlaunch.com/.

28 Finkle, J. (2019). *The introvert's complete guide: From landing a job to surviving, thriving, and moving on up*. Career Press, pp. 100–101.

29 Roepe, L.R. (n.d.). "What does the pandemic mean for your job search?" *The Muse*. http://morphpivotlaunch.com/.

30 WebFX. (2019, November 19). "6 best social media platforms for business." http://morphpivotlaunch.com/.

31 Roepe, L.R. (n.d.). "What does the pandemic mean for your job search?" *The Muse*. http://morphpivotlaunch.com/.

32 Pajer, N. (2020, March 21). "40 ways to stay social during the quarantine." *Parade*. http://morphpivotlaunch.com/.

33 Alterman, E. (2018, May 16). "This is how I talked to my kids about losing my job." *Fast Company*. http://morphpivotlaunch.com/.

34 Nix-Bloomer, C. (2020, April 17). Personal communication.

35 Lyons, S. (2020, January 23). "The bad outweighs the good: When it's time for a new job." *Forbes*. http://morphpivotlaunch.com/.

36 Carrick, M., & Dunaway, C. (2017). *Fit matters: How to love your job*. Maven House Press, pp. 11-12.

37 Guillebeau, C. (2017). *Side hustle: From idea to income in 27 days*. Crown Business, p. 31.

38 Burek, O. (2020, July 20). "40 easy ways to make money quickly." http://morphpivotlaunch.com/.

About the Authors

Deb Gaut

As a transformation and performance coach, Deb Gaut brings a genuine passion and vitality to helping others — particularly those who long to reconnect with their dreams and energize their careers. Her personal journey tells the tale of bold moves and successful transitions to pursue her own dreams — from academia to government to entrepreneurship. After 9/11 and 30+ years as a university professor, Deb decided to join the U.S. Department of Defense (DOD) in training and development for the next seven years. In both worlds, she enjoyed teaching and mentoring hundreds of people in the strategies, knowledge, and skills needed to effectively pursue their careers. During her time in academia, Deb co-authored three popular university textbooks in the field of Communication. "I am devoted to helping people leverage the remarkable power of visualization, mindset, and core energy to do what they really love," says Deb.

In 2017, Deb walked away from her six-figure position to become an entrepreneur. Today, in addition to her thriving coaching practice, she is the publisher of *Boomalally Magazine* (boomalally.com), an international speaker, and author of *Morph, Pivot, Launch*. Deb holds a Ph.D. in Communication and three professional coaching certifications: Certified Professional Coach (CPC), Energy Leadership Index — Master Practitioner (ELI-MP), and COR.E Dynamics — Transitions Specialist.

Her forever home is Saint Louis, Missouri, where she lives with her amazing husband and two four-legged children. To connect with Deb directly, reach out via LinkedIn at linkedin.com/in/deborah-gaut/ or go to MorphPivotLaunch.com.

Bonnie Sales

Bonnie Sales is an award-winning contemporary artist who is currently traveling, exploring, and creating in the Great Smoky Mountains, USA. In addition to her whimsical pencil drawings, she loves working in a wide variety of art forms — from watercolor, oil, and mural painting to wood carving, stained glass, jewelry making, and functional art. Originally from Cincinnati, Ohio, Bonnie inspires others to see life as a colorful journey filled with vibrance, joy, and contentment. Her talents have taken her to Jalisco, Mexico, where she created nine large murals and developed a love for bright colors and organic design. Perhaps the following excerpt from her artist statement best captures Bonnie's passion and purpose: "In a world where we sometimes forget to see the beauty in the mundane, my desire is to gift the viewer with a chance to be carried away in their own imagination: a place to dream, a unique world where all is well and cake is good for you!" You can learn more about Bonnie and view more of her beautiful artwork at HoneybeeArtCo.com.

Made in the USA
Las Vegas, NV
13 April 2021